Mercy and the Sufficiency of Grace

"Surely goodness and mercy shall follow me all
the days of my life."
—Psalms 23a

Fidel M. Donaldson

To: Colleen Morgan

God bless You

Shalom

Fidel M. Donaldson

03- 05- 18

TABLE OF CONTENTS

FOREWORD vii

AUTHOR'S NOTE ix

CHAPTER 1 MERCY 1

CHAPTER 2 THE SUFFICIENCY OF GRACE 21

CHAPTER 3 WANTED LIVING FAITH 33

CHAPTER 4 THE BLOOD OF JESUS CHRIST: THE LAMB OF GOD 45

CHAPTER 5 THE CHURCH 59

CHAPTER 6 THE POWER OF THE HOLY SPIRIT 79

CHAPTER 7 HAVE YOU LOST YOUR MIND? 89

CHAPTER 8 DON'T DIE IN THE WILDERNESS 97

ENDNOTES 105

BIBLIOGRAPHY 107

This book is dedicated to King Jesus.

Much Love To:

My wife for life Paulette Donaldson,
To: Dickey, Rickey, Link, Gary, Lance, Reggae Tierra,
Makeda, Mario Malik, Shante.

I give God the glory for all the great men and women who have
made a deposit in my life. Bishop James & Dr. Lillian C.
Ferguson, Dr. Samuel N. Greene, Prophet Andre Cook,
Pastors Arthur and Pauline Wade.

FOREWORD

If ever there was a time to hear the scriptures loudly declared—GOD is merciful, gracious, full of loving kindness, and tender mercies—it is surely now. Paul said, *"in my flesh dwelleth no good thing"* (Romans 7:18). He also said, *"the things I want to do, I can't seem to do; and the things I don't want to do, I end up doing. Who shall deliver me from this body of death? I thank GOD it's through Jesus"* (Romans 7:24). Only Jesus, only in Him, can we find hope, salvation, deliverance, restoration, and redemption. He has promised a people that He would "conform them to His image." He said, *"be perfect as I am perfect . . . be holy as I am holy."* He also said, *"I will redeem my people from all iniquity . . . I will thoroughly purge their sins that they may offer an offering in righteousness."* Paul said, *"Let us go on to perfection . . . that ye being complete in Him . . . it's no longer I that liveth, but Christ liveth in me...My little children of whom I travail in birth until Christ be formed in you..."*

GOD would not say these things to us if He could not give us the means for it to happen.

But in order for us to begin the journey to holiness, there must first be a true, pure, and enlightening revelation of God's grace and mercy. This wonderful and revelational book, written by my friend and fellow pastor, Fidel Donaldson, is the very one. It will introduce these great foundational truths regarding His grace and amazing mercy into your life. This book will change your life; it will alter your image of GOD and start you on your journey into Him.

When GOD declared to Moses who He was, His first words were, *"I am the Lord, the Lord GOD, merciful..."* This is truly our Father. Oh, that everyone would have this truth embedded in his or her conscience. The devil would be less important in our lives.

We would stop spending our lives in fear and condemnation, and embrace Him and His great love for us.

This book will help you tremendously. Read it, study it, believe it, and live it! Watch your life become more and more free. *"Stand fast in the liberty wherewith Christ hath made you free, and be not entangled in the yoke of bondage" (Galatians 5:1)*

May GOD get great glory out of this wonderful book!

Jesus Is Precious!
Dr. Samuel N. Greene

AUTHOR'S NOTE

The purpose of this book is to show the reader, through Biblical exposition, that our Heavenly Father is a God of mercy and grace. He desires all men to repent of their sins and enter into eternal life through Jesus Christ, His Son.

Many individuals have a misconception of God, which comes from ignorance or erroneous teachings. These misconceptions or teachings keep them from enjoying the benefits that flow from a committed relationship with Jesus. They see God as some cosmic bully who is waiting to cast them into a fiery place called Hell, where there will be eternal torment. This view of God causes many people to use salvation as fire insurance and a way to avoid wrath and judgment instead of using it as a vehicle that carries them on their journey to sanctification. Preachers don't need to scare the hell out of people; they need to draw the sinner to Jesus through love and kindness.

Webster's Collegiate Dictionary defines mercy as:
- Compassionate or kindly forbearance shown toward an offender, or an enemy
- Compassion or benevolence
- An act of kindness or favor

In no way am I suggesting that sin will go unpunished. God's righteousness demands that sinners be judged, but we must never forget that His judgment is an outflow of his righteousness. Before He sends judgment, He gives many opportunities for repentance.

How many times have you heard someone say, "I have to quit smoking, drinking, gambling etc... before I can go to church or before I can get saved"? How many times have you heard someone say, "God can't love me because of what I have done"? I believe the Prophet Isaiah has the best answer for those individuals trying to assess their state through reason. He wrote, *"Come now, and let us reason together, saith the LORD: though your sins be as scarlet, they shall be as white as snow; though they be red like crimson, they shall be as wool"* (Isaiah 1:18).

I want to state emphatically and unequivocally that if we could quit all our vices, God would not have needed to send Jesus to die in our place. We cannot clean ourselves up any more than a newborn baby can cleanse himself or herself. We are not simply dealing with bad habits—although we have many; the root of the problem is sin. King David said, *"Behold, I was shaped in iniquity; and in sin did my mother conceive me"* (Psalm 51:5).

The root of our problem is a sinful nature inherited from our progenitor, Adam. He disobeyed God and caused sin to enter into the human race, and with sin, death. It is not uncommon for people to ask the question, "If there is a God, why is there so much evil in the world?" Evil in the world does not negate the existence of God. It proves that human beings have no inherent righteousness or power to stop sinning. They are born with a nature that leads to a proclivity to commit ungodly acts. Some of the nicest people we know are capable of committing the vilest acts. We see the outward appearance, but God knows the heart. Oftentimes, people who attempt to justify their deeds or actions will say, "God knows my heart." However, the purpose of this statement is to give the impression that their actions are not representative of who they really are.

Actually, the opposite is true; whatever is on the inside will show up on the outside. *"For as he thinketh in his heart, so is he." (Proverbs 23:7a).* The Prophet Jeremiah said, *"The heart is deceitful above all things, and desperately wicked: who can know it?"* (Jeremiah 17:9). God knows all of the hidden things of the heart. No matter how one tries to hide or masquerade them, eventually they will manifest. Philippians 4:8 states: *"Finally, brethren, whatsoever things are true, whatsoever things are honest, whatsoever things are just, whatsoever things are pure, whatsoever things are lovely, whatsoever things are of good report; if there be any virtue, and if there be any praise, think on these things."* Without the transforming power of the Lord Jesus, we will always succumb to the carnal inclinations of our hearts.

We are totally dependent on the mercies of God to draw our next breath. Religion will lead us to believe there is some type of work we can do to gain a right standing with God. Jesus said, "We can do nothing without Him." Jesus said His disciples can't do anything without Him, so unbelievers need to realize how much they need Him.

CHAPTER 1
MERCY

The Apostle Paul wrote, *"for when we were yet without strength, in due time Christ died for the ungodly. For scarcely for a righteous man will one die: yet peradventure for a good man some would even dare to die. But God commendeth his love toward us, in that, while we were yet sinners, Christ died for us"* (Romans 5:6–8).

Paul tells us that at a set time, or *Kairos* moment, God chose to extend His mercy towards a weak, sinful people who deserved death. He did it by sending Jesus to die on the cross for our sins. Ask yourself this question: "Would I give up my only son or daughter for a murderer, a rapist, a thief, or a liar?" Most of us would be repulsed at the very thought of giving up something so precious for something so repulsive. We would be more inclined to call for the destruction of the thing that is offensive to us.

The natural mind cannot comprehend the depths of God's mercy, because we want to see transgressors punished swiftly and severely—as long as the transgressor is not someone, we love. Asaph wrote, *"Truly God is good to Israel, even to such as are of a clean heart. But as for me, my feet were almost gone; my steps had well nigh slipped for I was envious at the foolish, when I saw the prosperity of the wicked"* (Psalm 73:1–3). God extends mercy so the transgressor can come to Him and receive a pardon. We have nothing of value to offer God for the debt we owe. God loves us so much He paid the debt for us. God's righteousness demands that sinners be judged, so no sin can go unpunished. It might appear as if the sinner has cheated death, but at a given time, or a due time, everyone will have to give an account to Jesus.

The due time normally occurs when a person's back is against the wall and there is a sense of hopelessness. She comes to the

1

end of the road and begins to look outside herself for a solution to her crisis. For some, it could be a matter of life and death. For others, it could be a drug addiction that has plagued them for years, causing great pain and suffering. It could be in a prison cell where the inmate has spent many years trapped because he could not free himself from a desire to indulge in criminal activity. It could be a place where an individual is contemplating suicide. Whatever the situation, the mercy of God is there and available in abundance.

Gene Cunningham states, *"God's mercy withholds from us what we deserve. Because God judged Jesus Christ on the cross for all our sins, He can offer us mercy. He can also offer us grace. God's grace gives us what we do not deserve—the righteousness of Jesus Christ, the riches of His glory, inheritance, power, and much more. But the only people who can lay hold of grace are those who realize their need for mercy."*[1]

In order to lay hold of what we do not deserve, God must free us from what we deserve. Because of our propensity to commit sin, we deserve death. But God's mercy stops the execution long enough for us to receive His grace, which is exactly what we did not deserve. Mercy and grace find their perfect expression in the redemptive work of Jesus at Calvary. His vicarious and atoning death paid our sin debt and opened the door for God's unmerited favor in our lives. This is not done out of pity; it is done because God loves us.

The Bible says, *"The Word was made flesh and dwelt among us"* (John 1:14). The purpose of this was two-fold: first, to destroy the works of darkness, and second, to offer salvation to all who repent. The type of people to whom Jesus ministered is proof that God is no respecter of persons. He chose a cussing fisherman who pulled a sword on someone and cut his ear off; He chose a despised tax collector who overcharged people, and a treasurer who stole from the treasury and wound up selling him out for thirty pieces of silver. He was criticized for ministering to wine bibbers and the outcasts of society. Jesus wants all transgressors to experience the Father's mercy.

A friend of mine once described himself as an alley cat that Jesus made into an aristocrat. I think that is a good way to describe what Jesus did for us. When we were at our lowest point and bound by an ungodly lifestyle, God sent Jesus to die for us. It is imperative that every believer, especially those ordained to the five-fold ministry, be as transparent as possible; that the light of Jesus can shine and give light to those trapped in darkness. The only mercy most people will see, is the Godly mercy, which emanates from born again believers. We should be ready and willing to testify about the sinful lifestyle from which Jesus delivered us. If we as believers act as though we have never sinned, how then will unbelievers know that God can pardon their sins? Jesus said, *"Let your light so shine before men, that they may see your good works, and glorify your Father which is in heaven"* (Matthew 5:16). Jesus is not referring to some religious duty done to gain heavenly points. It is a labor of love among the poor, the broken, and the rejected. By our Godly actions toward those who cannot repay us, we show the wonderful light of mercy that emanates from His throne.

Many modern day priests and Levites are religiously callous. They pass by the suffering individual on the road of sin and degradation, unable to empathize with them. They enter their beautiful houses of worship, oblivious to the fact that the greatest worship we can give Jesus is to show mercy and serve the least of his people. The Lord has given every believer a talent, or talents. He expects us to invest those talents wisely so the Kingdom can be established. The Kingdom is the sovereign rule and reign of the Lord Jesus in the lives of people. Jesus expects to receive a return on the talents He has invested in us. The Bible is explicit in its description of the individual who is slothful with his talent. Jesus said, *"And cast the unprofitable servant into outer darkness: There will be weeping and gnashing of teeth"* (Matthew 25:30). We must resist the desire to shut ourselves up in our places of worship, fellowshipping with individuals who are familiar to us. Jesus has called us into the highways and the hedges. Are you willing to roll up your sleeves and get in the trenches to reach the ungodly that are without spiritual strength?

There was a time in my life when I was without strength—a time when I lived an ungodly lifestyle, which landed me in a prison cell in England. It was a time when I needed God's mercy. I remember vividly those precious Christians who took the time to visit the prison and share the love of Jesus with me. I saw God's mercy in action through the love they shared. Many believers have become aloof and disconnected from the masses. Personally, I know some believers who have stopped fellowshipping with other believers whom they consider to be beneath their level. Can the servant be greater than his master? If they treat another believer like that, how will they treat an unbeliever?

According to the Apostle Paul, people will scarcely die for a righteous man, and some would die for a good man, but God proved His love for us by sending Jesus to die on the cross. God knows the deplorable and sinful state of each human being, no matter how expensive the costume or how sweet the perfume. He is able to look beyond the façade, and at the most opportune time, He extends His love through mercy and grace to free man from his sins.

"In due time" is a phrase that intrigues me. Two of the Greek words used in the New Testament to describe time are, *Chronos* and *Kairos*. *Vine's Dictionary of New Testament Words* states that *Chronos* denotes a space of time, whether short or long. For example:

Luke states, *"And they arrived at the country of the Gadarenes, which is over against Galilee and when he went forth to land there met him out of the city a certain man, which had devils a **long time**, and wore no clothes, neither abode in any house, but in the tombs"* (Luke 8:26–27). The demoniac of the Gadarenes was possessed by devils for a long duration of time. No close signifies he had no covering, no house means lack of a connection to family or a loving home, and the tombs represent him being in a place of death. He was living among the dead. This paints a picture of sinners in the world who are akin to dead men walking.

Kairos refers to a season, a period possessed of certain characteristics. For example, Luke states, *"And when the devil had ended all the temptation, he departed from him for a season"* (Luke 4:13), or a more opportune time. *Chronos* normally denotes quantity while *Kairos* denotes quality. We might experience trials for a long time; then, at a set time, Jesus will bring deliverance to our situation.

Like the demoniac from the Gadarenes, the sinner is *passing time* in a tomb of sin, without strength, trapped in an ungodly lifestyle. He or she might not exhibit the radical characteristics of demon possession like the demoniac. He ripped his clothes and broke the chains that confined him. Modern day sinners use material things to cover themselves and give the impression that

4

all is well. However, like the demoniac, the sinner needs a *Kairos* or timely visit from Jesus to loose him from the power and penalty of sin. The demoniac was able to break the man-made chains, but only Jesus can break the chains that bind the unbeliever.

The Holy Spirit illuminated Romans 5:8 when I was returning home after a service several years ago. He opened my eyes so I could see how sinners without strength are desperately in need of the love of Jesus. I was looking out of the window of the car in which I was riding. My attention was drawn to the people outside because I knew many of them. I wondered if most of them realized it was the mercy of God why they were not consumed. As I pondered that thought in my heart, the Holy Spirit said to me, "You didn't get what you deserved." It was easy for me to think there was some blessing due to me, which I did not receive, and God was about to intervene on my behalf to correct the oversight. At that moment, the Spirit of the Lord began to deal with me heavily concerning God's mercy and grace.

Many of the individuals I saw that Sunday afternoon were addicted to alcohol and drugs; caught up in a lifestyle that was not pleasing to God. It would have been easy for me to look at those people with disdain and contempt because I was better off than many of them. But the Lord reminded me of a time when I, too, was milling about those same streets in pursuit of sinful pleasures. He reminded me that it was because of His mercies that I did not die from the drugs, alcohol, and gang violence that had taken so many lives in the neighborhood.

Just a few years before that Sunday afternoon, I was a gun toting, drug dealing, and alcohol-drinking thug. I hung out with gangsters who would kill anyone who invaded their turf. Remembering the death and lengthy prison sentences of many of the individuals I called "friends" makes me appreciate how God's mercy spared my life. My life was not spared because I was special and they were not—God is sovereign, and His actions flow from His sovereignty.

God told Moses, *"I will make all my goodness pass before thee, and I will proclaim the name of the Lord before thee; and will be gracious to whom I will be gracious, and will show mercy on whom I will show mercy"* (Exodus 33:19). Moses killed an Egyptian and fled the scene of the crime, but God showed him mercy and used him mightily. I knew if God could do it for a wretched sinner like me, surely He could do it for those individuals in the streets who were like zombies. They were like fiends hunting their next hit of crack, heroin, or Night Train (the cheap wine bums drink). I was certain the answer to the scourge of drug and alcohol addiction that plagued those people was the Lord Jesus.

We all know people whom God has delivered from certain situations. I was one of those people. He would not allow me to act as if I was better them. As soon as I had an inclination to act as though I was better, He would say to me, *"Remember the pig pen?"* He did not have to finish the sentence, because my mind would go immediately to the time of my arrest in England for drug smuggling. After a year on remand, I received an eight-year prison sentence. My mother always told me money earned from the selling of illicit drugs was blood money, and one day I would have to give an account for my deeds. However, when you have thousands of dollars readily available, wear the finest clothes, and have women to pick from, you disregard people who warn you of coming destruction.

My Testimony

I was sent to Wormwood Scrubs to await trial for conspiracy to smuggle drugs into England. I was locked in a cell with another inmate for 23 hours a day. The prison was a very old facility with no toilet in the cell, and if you came down with a bad case of diarrhea during the night, you were at the mercy of the guards. It was not uncommon for a new inmate to be brought to the cell in the middle of the night, because inmates were constantly going to court.

Twenty-three hours in a cell, half the size of most people's bedroom can lead to a serious case of claustrophobia. The problem was exacerbated by the fact that those small quarters had to be shared by two people. The cellmates were not choirboys; they were usually hardened criminals, so I would have to sleep with one eye open. A fellow inmate once told me that another inmate, with whom he shared a cell, started a fire in the cell. He awakened to the smell of smoke. The inmate who lit the cell on fire had a bed sheet wrapped around his head. The guy was obviously deranged.

I spent time reading magazines and exercising, but that did not ease the pain of the separation from my wife and children. Nor did it remove the mental anguish of the possibility of a lengthy prison sentence. I became more agitated when I found out I was named an un-indicted co-conspirator in an organized crime syndicate in Junction City, Kansas. I was visited by some English detectives who told me they were in contact with officers in the NYPD. They stated that if I gave them some information, I could be given a lighter sentence. I told them I was not an informant, I was willing to do every day of any sentence I was given, and, if someone messed with me inside, I was willing to kill them. The officers left after they realized I was not interested.

I found a small Gideon's Bible in the dresser drawer next to my bed, and for the first time in my life, I began to read the Bible for myself. I read Matthew to The Revelation several times. On March 6, 1991, I was reading John Chapter 5 when the words finally began to pierce my heart. It wasn't the first time I'd read that chapter, but this time there was something different. At the time, I did not know the Holy Spirit was convicting me of sin and drawing me to Jesus.

John Chapter 5 records the healing of the lame man at the pool called Be-thes-da. It is called Be-thes-da because it has five porches. It is important to note that the number five in scripture represents grace. *Be-thes-da* means "house of mercy." In retrospect, I now see how God's grace and mercy worked together to bring me to Jesus.

There were many people at the pool who were sick. John 5:3 states, *"In these lay a great multitude of impotent folk, of blind, halt, withered, waiting for the moving of the water. For an angel went down at a certain season into the pool, and troubled the water: whosoever then first after the troubling of the water stepped in was made whole of whatsoever disease he had."*

Verse 5 says, *"And a certain man was there which had an infirmity thirty and eight years."* Thirty represents preparation for ministry, and eight represents new beginnings. When Jesus saw him lying there, and knew that he had been there a long time in that condition, He asked the man if he wanted to be made whole. The man wanted to give Jesus a long story, but Jesus cut to the chase and told him, *"Rise, take up thy bed, and walk."* The Bible says the

7

man was made whole immediately. Beloved, it does not matter how long you have been battling your current infirmity. Please do not become weary because Jesus is still troubling the water and bringing healing.

Jesus came under serious persecution because He healed the man on the Sabbath. The religious zealots actually tried to kill Jesus. Jesus' response was, *"My Father has been working until now, and I have been working"* (John 5:17 NKJV). The religious folks who were incensed by his response tried harder to kill Jesus:

For the first time in my life, I began to hear the voice of Jesus. I came under deep conviction when I read these words, *"Then answered Jesus and said unto them, Verily, verily, I say unto you, The Son can do nothing of himself, but what he seeth the Father do: for what things soever he doeth, these also doeth the Son likewise (John 5:19).*

There was an epic struggle-taking place in my soul as I pondered the claims Jesus was making about Himself. For most of my adult life, I was a black nationalist who had espoused the teachings of Malcolm X and the Honorable Marcus Mosiah Garvey. Although my grandparents were devout Christians, I had denied Christianity, categorically, as a way of life for myself. I could not get past the picture of the longhaired white man I saw hanging in many homes and many churches. I always thought he could not be God because he looked like some of the white people who had chased me growing up and called me NIGGER. The "five percenters" always told me that the white man was the devil; the Muslims told me the Jews had corrupted the scriptures; and the Rastafarians told me Emperor Haile Selassie was God, and King James, and Shakespeare had written the Bible.

Now I was alone with the Bible and hearing the voice of the real Jesus. I knew it was the real Jesus because there was no preacher in the cell with me, no church choir, and no wife telling me I needed to give my heart to the Lord—but something was happening to me. Jesus was saying I had to accept Him to escape damnation and receive everlasting life. I remember crying out, "What does one man dying on the cross have to do with me personally?" A soft voice spoke to the depths of my soul and said, "Take every filthy sin you have ever committed and put it on Him." I knew I had done some terrible, vile acts. The voice went on to say, "Don't stop there, take every sin committed by your mother, father, children, and put them on Him."

I began to weep in my cell as the thoughts of the filthy life I had lived flooded my soul. There was another voice trying to convince me that I could not live for Jesus because I was in prison, and what was I going to do once I came out and no one hired me? I ignored that voice because I realized that I might not make it out of that wretched place. I knew at that moment that there was a Divine Presence in the cell with me, and I wanted the forgiveness and cleansing He provided.

I remembered there was a part in the Gideon's Bible that told you how to ask Jesus into your heart. I knelt, turned to the page, and told Jesus I was a sinner. I told him I believed He shed His blood for my sins, and I wanted Him to come into my life and be my savior. Words cannot adequately describe the peace and joy that filled my soul, but suffice it to say, my dark soul lit up with the light of the Lord Jesus. Instantly, I went from darkness into His marvelous light! The mental anguish I feared was eradicated immediately. Hallelujah!! There was a fire lit under me, and I could not wait for the cell doors to open so I could begin to be a witness for Jesus. I realized that I was a dead man who had received a pardon, and I wanted to reach other dead men to tell them that the Word became flesh and died on the cross for their sins, so they could have eternal life through Jesus Christ.

I witnessed in the prison with boldness. I started a Bible study in my cell and many inmates were touched by the power of God. I saw first-hand how the power of God transformed the lives of hardened criminals. It is an amazing transformation when a Prodigal Son comes to himself and realizes God is merciful and His grace is sufficient. If you are not saved, take a moment now, confess your sins, and ask Jesus to come into your heart.

Earlier, I mentioned how God delivers people from certain situations. Swaleside was the name of the prison I was sent to after my conviction. It was located on the Isle of Sheppy, next to a pig farm. When the wind blew, the stench from the pigs would permeate my cell and practically suffocate me. If you think hospital food is bad, then you should try eating some of the slop served in prison. I ate a great deal oatmeal because I found it more palatable. You can imagine how devastated I was when a fellow inmate told me that on the bags of oatmeal that I loved so much was a stamp that read, "Pigs meal." The inmates had to eat the same oatmeal that was used to fatten the pigs.

9

My experience on the Isle of Sheppy left an indelible impression on my psyche. I was stripped of my fancy clothes, I had no champagne to drink, and there were no women, just a bunch of violent males. I was a number and had to march to the beat of the prison guards. They told me when to eat, and when to sleep. It became very clear to me that a man without Jesus is like a pig wallowing in a sty.

The Prodigal Son

One of the best examples of the mercy and grace of our Heavenly Father is found in the story of the prodigal son. *Luke 15:11–32*, The younger of two sons came to his father and requested his father give him the portion of inheritance, which was his. It was an unusual request, because the older son was in line to get his inheritance first, and that would happen when the father was about to die. The Bible says the father divided his possessions among them. The older son stayed home, but the younger son gathered all his things and traveled to a far country, and there wasted his substance with riotous living.

Let's exegete this first portion of the text: The younger son represents the gentiles that moved away from God. By contrast, the older brother represents a Pharisaical and religious people, bound by legalism and the traditions of men. Please take notice of the fact that the younger son took all his things, showing his desire to sever all ties to his father's house. This point is reinforced when we examine his destination and the purpose of his trip. He took his journey into a far country and wasted his substance with riotous living. It would appear that he wanted to be as far from his father's house as possible. He was willing to remove himself from his covering in order to indulge in the fulfillment of the lust of the flesh. Many young people say they cannot wait until they turn 18 so they can leave their parents home. If they knew what awaited them, they would stay home as long as possible.

After he spent everything, a mighty famine arose and he had nothing left for sustenance. It is one thing to have no sustenance when there is a famine, but it is worse when it is a mighty famine.

The Bible says he went to work for a citizen of the country in which he lived, and that individual sent him into his fields to feed swine. There is something very important to glean here. Jesus was speaking primarily to the Pharisees at this time. They were strict adherents to the Law of Moses, so swine was untouchable. Luke's description gives us a vivid picture of how far the younger son had fallen. He became so hungry that he desired to fill his belly with the husk that the swine ate, and no one would give him a meal. There is a spiritual aspect to this important verse. His physical hunger was a picture of his spiritual starvation, which was the result of removing himself from his father's house and covering. *Verse 17* captures beautifully the due time spoken of by the Apostle Paul in *Romans 5:6*.

It is an awesome revelation of the pivotal moment in time—that *Kairos* moment when an individual has reached the end of his human strength and comes to a realization that he needs the Father. Luke writes, *"And when he came to himself, he said, How many hired servants of my father's have bread enough and to spare, and I perish with hunger! I will arise and go to my father, and will say unto him, father, I have sinned against heaven, and before thee, and am no more worthy to be called thy son: make me as one of thy hired servants"* (Luke 15:17–19).

The first thing he had to do was come to himself. This simply means that he came to a realization of the wretchedness of his condition. The second thing he did was to remember that his father's house was a place of provision and abundance. It was such a place of provision that the servants had enough bread and some to spare. Every individual living outside the ark of safety needs to know that God has everything they stand in need of and more. Jesus is the bread that came down from Heaven to feed all who are hungry for salvation in His name.

When we were first introduced to this son, he was looking to get as far away from his father's house as he could. After tasting the fruit of riotous living, he is now ready to go back home—not as a son but as a servant. Beloved, you cannot attain to son-ship without a servant's heart. It is interesting to note that the hired servants in the father's house had bread enough to spare, but the natural son was perishing with hunger. Anytime we allow ourselves to be enticed away from the Father's house because of earthly goods, we can expect to perish both spiritually and physically.

The third thing he does after he comes to himself is to arise. Once God opens our eyes and we see that we are in a detestable condition, it's time to arise! Not with an attitude, or anger, but we must arise vengeance with a spirit of humility. He decides to go to his father and confess his sin, and inform his father that he is not worthy to be called a son, but a servant. He actually asked the father to make him one of the hired servants. When he first went to his father, his request was, "Father, give me." Now that he has been humbled by the pigsty, his new request is, "Father, make me." This should be the cry of every individual.

When he was a great way off, his father saw him. Although the younger son did not leave home in a positive manner, his father never stopped looking for him. We are never so far from our Heavenly Father's omnipresent eyes that He is unable to see us. He does not see us superficially, but He is able to peer into the inner chambers of our heart to discern true desire.

Now we see the mercy and grace of the Father shining like a glorious light. The father had compassion for him, and hugged and kissed him. God is not mad at His sons and daughters who mess up. He is not mad at people trapped in sin. His heart's desire is that they recognize their condition, repent, and head home to the Kingdom as a son or daughter.

Although the younger son had dishonored the father by taking his inheritance and wasting it, the father does not treat him like a hired servant when he returns. On the contrary Verses 22-23, describes the blessing he receives. *"But the father said to his servants, Bring forth the best robe, and put it on him; and put a ring on his hand, and shoes on his feet: And bring hither the fatted calf, and kill it; and let us eat, and be merry: For this my son was dead, and is alive again; he was lost, and is found. And they began to be merry."*

The best robe represents him being back under his chief covering. The ring on his hand represents a signet or a seal of son-ship. The shoes on his feet signified that his walk with his father was back in right standing. The killing of the fatted calf represented his father sacrificing the best for him. The merry celebration is indicative of the celebration that takes place in Heaven when a sinner is converted. It is important to note that repentance means more than saying I'm sorry. The Greek word for repentance is *met-an-o-eh-o*, which means, "to think differently." The younger son had to change the stinking thinking that led him to the pigsty, and so will the individual who does not know Jesus as Lord and Savior.

The adversary desires to deceive us into believing we can mess up and undo what God has for us, but this is not so. The Holy Spirit within us will draw us back to the Father no matter how far we have strayed, because greater is He that is in us than he that is in the world. The journey back to the Father is facilitated by the knowledge that He is waiting for His sons and daughters to return so He can get the heavenly party started. The younger son thought he had to go to a far country to get his groove on, but someone once said: *"Ain't no party like a Holy Ghost party, because a Holy Ghost party don't stop."*

With the introduction of the older brother, we see a self-righteous, jealous, and angry person. Luke 15:25–30: *"Now his elder son was in the field: and as he came and drew nigh to the house, he heard music and dancing. And he called one of the servants, and asked what these things meant. And he said unto him, Thy brother is come; and thy father hath killed the fatted calf, because he hath received him safe and sound. And he was angry, and would not go in: therefore came his father out, and intreated him. And he answering said to his father, Lo, these many years do I serve thee, neither transgressed I at any time thy commandment: and yet thou never gavest me a kid, that I might make merry with my friends: But as soon as this thy son was come, which hath devoured thy living with harlots, thou hast killed for him the fatted calf."*

The older brother had to ask the servants the reason for the celebration. He didn't leave the house like the younger brother, but the servants were more privy to the father's business than he was. Many people are in the church, but are ignorant of the father's business because they lack a servant's heart. His response when his father came out and entreated him is the same response given by people in the bondage of religion when the Holy Spirit visits them to touch their hearts and give them the mind of Jesus. His response was one of anger and a desire to obtain righteousness through works. He was quick to point out that he never transgressed any of the commandments, and his brother had wasted his father's money with harlots. False, hypocritical religion is one of the biggest hindrances to someone receiving salvation.

The older son is drawn to the house by the music and dancing; what a powerful indictment against the enemies of worship who level criticism against churches for praising the Lord with music and dancing. The son comes to the house from the field, and instead of going inside and joining the festivities, he asked one of the servants for an explanation. The text says he was angry and would not enter the house when he found out his wayward brother had returned home, and his father had killed the fatted calf.

How many believers are away from the presence of God because of jealousy and anger? His father came out and entreated him to join the festivities. "Entreated" in the Greek language is *Parakaleo*; it means, "to call near, to exhort, to invoke (by imploration, hortation or consolation)." It comes from the root "para," which means "beside," and "kaleo," which means, "to call aloud."

The father came out to the obstinate son as a comforter because Parakaleo comes from the same root as *parakletos*, which means "a comforter." Jesus uses this word when He told the disciples that the Father would give them another comforter. The father went to his son in the same manner in which the Holy Spirit comes to each person to draw them to Jesus. His response when his father came out and entreated him is the same response given by people in the bondage of religion when the Holy Spirit visits them to loose them from their religious mindset, so they can be free to worship God. The eldest son's rejection of the father's request to come in is akin to the rejection of the Holy Spirit by the religious mind-set that permeates many churches.

God's compassion for His people

"The Lord is merciful and gracious, slow to anger, and plenteous in mercy" (Psalm 103:8). It is important to know that every waking moment we live is attributable to the mercies of God. The prophet Jeremiah states it emphatically and explicitly in Lamentations 3:19–22: *"Remembering mine affliction and my misery, the wormwood and the gall. My soul hath them still in remembrance, and is humbled in me. This I recall to my mind, therefore have I hope. It is of the Lord's mercies that we are not consumed, because his compassions fail not. They are new every morning: great is thy faithfulness"*

The prophet remembers his affliction and misery and is humbled by them, but he is able to press on and be productive in God. He recalls something marvelous about God, and that something is, no matter how destructive the wormwood, or how bitter the gall, we must have hope because our merciful Father will not allow us to be consumed. The prophet said that God's compassions fail not. They are new every morning; great is His faithfulness. How comforting it is to know that when you go to bed every night, no matter what you have to face in the morning, once you wake up, God's compassion awaits you. What a mighty God we serve—a God that is so concerned with His people that He waits for them each day with compassion.

The awesome manifestation of His love for us moved King David to ask an important question in Psalm 8:3–4: *"When I consider thy heavens, the work of thy fingers, the moon and the stars, which thou hast ordained; What is man, that thou art mindful of him? and the son of man, that thou visitest him?"* God's mercy and love for His people moved David to ponder how the Almighty God, who created the heavens, the moon, and the stars, could be so concerned with His people that His mind would be full of thoughts concerning them. He acts upon these thoughts by visiting us every morning. We would be less stressed and tossed about if we remembered this fact.

It is the enemy's desire to get us so distracted with the cares of this life that we lose focus on the fact that we are the apple of God's eye. I remember the zeal and the fire that I had for the Lord when He saved me. I used to boast on Him so much that my sister-in-law once said, "He acts like God is His God only!" My response was, "I can't help it if He makes me feel like an only child." We must apply God's love personally to our lives.

Above all else, the God we serve is a God of mercy. In Matthew Chapter 9, Jesus comes under persecution for healing a man sick of the palsy. The persecution stemmed from the fact that Jesus told the sick man to be of good cheer because Jesus had forgiven his sins. The religious leaders began to think evil of Him because they felt He committed blasphemy when He forgave the man's sins. He came under further criticism when He sat down to eat with publicans and sinners. His response to them was, *"whole people do not need a physician but those who are sick."* He actually quotes Hosea 6:6: *"But go ye and learn what that meaneth. I will have mercy, and not sacrifice: for I am not come to call the righteous, but sinners to repentance."*

That statement must have angered the religious leaders, because the sacrifice was instituted by God under the Levitical priesthood to bring cleansing and forgiveness of sins to the people. The religious leaders of Jesus' day had made the sacrifices meaningless, because they had become an empty ritual, void of the central focus for which they had been instituted. The focus was supposed to be on God's unending mercy towards sinful man. The Lord does not want us to become so ritualistic in our services we forget to show mercy to those who do not know Him. The prophet Hosea paints a vivid picture of God's mercy by showing him as the Husbandman who cannot leave his wife (Israel), despite her sins. Micah 6:8 tells us that since we have received mercy, we should pass it on to others, and by doing so, we show that we love God with action and not just lip service.

The true wish of God is not ceremonies or religious works, according to Hosea 6:8, but mercy shown to others; this is the expectation from God for those He has redeemed. The tendency in some secular and religious circles is to view the God of the Old Testament as a God of Judgment. I submit to you that from the very beginning of his dealings with men, God has always been merciful.

It is no coincidence that the name of the seat from which the Lord communed with the nation of Israel was the Mercy Seat. In Genesis 25:17a, God instructs Moses to make a mercy seat of pure gold. Gold represents His deity, and the purity of the gold represents the fact that His mercy would flow from a source that is not diluted or polluted. Verses 21-22 read: *"And thou shalt put the mercy seat above upon the ark; and in the ark thou shalt put the testimony that I shall give thee and there I will meet with thee, and I will commune with thee from above the mercy seat, from between the two cherubims which are upon the ark of the testimony, of all things which I will give thee in commandment unto the children of Israel."*

The word Ark conjures up images of safety and security. We see a beautiful picture of this recorded in Exodus 2. Moses' mother placed him in an ark to protect him from Pharaoh in-order to spare his life. The Mercy Seat was placed above the Ark because His mercy is the thing that facilitates our escape from judgment and wrath and allows us to enter into the Ark, where we can have sweet communion and fellowship with Him. He communes with us from a place of mercy, because without His mercy, there is no communion or fellowship. It is important to understand that the Ark is none other than the Lord Jesus. He is the door that gives us entrance to the sweet presence of God.

According to *John 1:17*, the law was given to Moses but grace and truth came by the Lord Jesus. This scripture in no way negates the fact that God has always shown mercy to mankind Here are a few examples: In *Genesis 3:21*, the Lord made a coat of skins to cover Adam and his wife Eve after their disobedience gave them a conscious awareness of sin. In Genesis 4:15, he set a mercy mark on their son Cain after he had slain his brother Abel so Cain would not be murdered by men seeking vengeance. In *Genesis 6:8, "Noah found grace in the eyes of the Lord."* God was getting ready to send a flood upon the earth because all flesh had become corrupt. Man had obviously reached a state in which he had rejected all calls to repent and turn from wickedness.

The first time we see the word mercy in the Bible, it is in reference to Lot and his family escaping from the cities of Sodom. It is not the first instance of God being merciful but the first instance of the use of the word mercy. Lot had departed from his uncle and spiritual covering, Abram, and had pitched his tent towards Sodom because the surrounding land was very fertile. The grass may look greener on the other side but we must be careful we don't get stuck in mud, because looks are deceiving. Genesis 13:13 reads: *"But the men of Sodom were wicked and sinners before the Lord exceeding."* The men were not only sinners; they were also wicked and exceedingly so. At a certain point in time, their sinfulness came before the Lord for judgment. Abram interceded for Lot, and the Lord sent two angels to the city to remove Lot and his family.

"And it came to pass, when they had brought them forth abroad, that he said, Escape for thy life; look not behind thee, neither stay thou in all the plain; escape to the mountain, lest thou be consumed" (Genesis 19:17–22). What a beautiful picture of how God made a way of escape for Lot and his family. I believe the mountain God has provided for every individual who is perishing is none other than Jesus Christ. When we think of a mountain, we think of climbing and going up. Lot does not seem eager to follow the plan as the angels gave it to him. Verses 18 and 19 read, *"And Lot said unto them, Oh, not so, my Lord: Behold now, thy servant hath found grace in thy sight, and thou hast magnified thy mercy, which thou hast shewed unto me in saving my life;*

and I cannot escape to the mountain, lest some evil take me, and I die."

He readily admits that he has found Grace in God's sight and mercy magnified in the saving of his life, but he believes he will be overtaken by evil if he flees to the mountain. Why would God provide Grace and Mercy only to lead him to a mountain where evil would overtake him? Lot had no desire to distance himself from the plain of Jordan where Sodom and Gomorrah was located. Let us examine his request to the angels as recorded in Verses 20 and 22:

"Behold now, this city is near to flee unto, and it is a little one: Oh, let me escape thither, (is it not a little one?) And my soul shall live. And he said unto him, See, I have accepted thee concerning this thing also, that I will not overthrow this city, for the reason which thou hast spoken. Haste thee, escape thither; for I cannot do any thing till thou be come thither. Therefore the name of the city was called Zoar."

Why would Lot settle for a little city when God was giving him a mountain? The word *Zoar* means "little, to be small, to be brought low." Lot told the angels that if they allowed him to go to Zoar, his soul would live. Lot was thinking small because the soul is the seat of the intellect, the will, and the emotions. Why would he settle for his soul to live in a small, ignoble place when his spirit could grow in the mountain God was willing to give him? Eventually Lot would leave the city of Zoar for the mountain, but it was not because he was heeding the word of the Lord. It was because of fear. He winds up dwelling in a cave with his two daughters, which led to an incestuous relationship that produced the nations of Moab and Ammon. We must never settle for God's mercy and grace solely as conduits out of a place of wrath; we must understand that He brings us out to perfect us so His glory will manifest in and through us.

Because of His mercy, He is able to look beyond our faults to identify our need. All our faults stem from the need in our lives. Once we yield to God and allow Him to fill the need, the met need will help us overcome all our faults. The greatest need of every human is the need of a Savior who could restore the breach and bring us back into unity and fellowship with God. Beloved, the Savior is the Lord Jesus Christ and no other.

Many people have been deceived into thinking their good works can get them into a right relationship with God. A coworker at my former work place once asked me why so many innocent people die if there is a God. I told her that if God were to start judging sin at that moment, she would not be sitting there. She was under the misguided impression that because she had not killed or robbed anyone, she was somehow more deserving of life than the hardened criminals we see on the evening news and on shows like *Cops* and *Americas Most Wanted*. If we would be honest with ourselves, we would realize that all unregenerate human beings are on God's most wanted list, and mercy is what keeps them alive.

My co-worker failed to understand that we are living in a fallen world inhabited by fallen people, and the ensuing result is sin. It is the gateway into our lives for death and destruction. Death and destruction do not discriminate based on age, sex, or race. On the contrary, they can choose to visit any one from the aforementioned groups because all people have one thing in common: We were all born in sin and shaped in iniquity. Yes, even that cute little bouncy baby that you adore was born with a nature that makes him or her prone to do that which is bad. You don't have to teach a young child to lie or to steal. You have to teach him the exact opposite, because there is a nature in him that predisposes him towards negative behaviors—some more terrible than others. All have the propensity to commit vile and sadistic acts. We must take the blinders off and realize that our feeble attempt at righteousness without Jesus Christ does not impress God.

Do you really want to know what God thinks about man's righteousness? Listen to what the Prophet Isaiah wrote concerning the goodness of man: *"But we are all as an unclean thing, and all our righteousness are as filthy rags; and we all do fade as a leaf; and our iniquities, like the wind, have taken us away" (Isaiah 64:6).*

When the prophet says our righteousness is as filthy rags, he is not talking about the rags we use to clean our homes. In the Hebrew version, we get a very graphic description of what the prophet meant. Gene Cunningham writes, "In the Hebrew, *Isaiah 64:6* is graphic in its description of the good that man can produce." All our righteousness, it says, is as the rag of a menstruous woman. Cunningham goes on to ask the question, "Why would the Holy Spirit inspire Isaiah to use this particular analogy?" The answer he gives is this: "Because the flow of blood in the menstrual cycle is evidence that there has been no conception. No conception means there will be no birth, and no birth means no life. Isaiah is saying that all human good is dead in God's sight."[2] No one is exempt from the analogy given by the prophet Isaiah. No matter how good and righteous the individual thinks, he is; his righteousness without Christ is as a filthy rag.

CHAPTER 2
THE SUFFICIENCY OF GRACE

"*And lest I should be exalted above measure through the abundance of the revelations, there was given to me a thorn in the flesh, the messenger of Satan to buffet me, lest I should be exalted above measure. For this thing I besought the Lord thrice, that it might depart from me. And he said unto me, My grace is sufficient for thee: for my strength is made perfect in weakness. Most gladly therefore will I rather glory in my infirmities, that the power of Christ may rest upon me. Therefore I take pleasure in infirmities, in reproaches, in necessities, in persecutions, in distresses for Christ's sake: for when I am weak, then am I strong" (2 Corinthians 12:7–10).*

Webster's Collegiate Dictionary defines Grace as, a manifestation of favor, especially by a superior. The freely given, unmerited favor, and love of God, the influence or spirit of God operating in humans. "The essence of grace is that it is an undeserved gift of God. The very life Jesus lived was a gift of God to a sin-weary world. Love, grace, and mercy are an inseparable trinity in God's dealing with mankind." For the love of God to be poured out to sinful and undeserving man, His mercy must subtract our sin through forgiveness, and His grace must add what we lack—eternal life and the righteousness of Christ. Mercy takes away the judgment we richly deserve, while grace provides us with the blessings that we do not deserve. Everything in His earthly life spoke of the sacrificial love of God and His desire to bless His creatures. The matchless grace of God would accomplish what the Law of Moses never could.[3]

The thorn in the flesh that plagued the Apostle Paul was serious enough for him to seek the Lord three times for its alleviation. Some theologians have surmised that the thorn was some malady of the eye, but proper hermeneutics demand that the Bible be the first interpreter of itself. The Apostle tells us what the thorn is. It is the messenger of Satan sent to buffet him. Gene Cunningham writes, "Paul was under tremendous attack by the carnal, critical, judgmental Christians in Corinth, who were letting the things they did not find attractive about the apostle distract them from the message he carried. The theme running all the way through the book is that it's always the message, and never the man who delivers the message. That is the issue, that God devised a way to use imperfect people as vehicles for a perfect message. So important is this that Paul states it twice in verse seven with the phrase 'Lest I be exalted above measure.' God knew that when he poured the power of His Word through Paul there would be a very great danger that Paul would be tempted to magnify his importance. So God allowed what was apparently a high-ranking demon to be assigned to the apostle to inflict bodily pain and damage on him. He calls it 'a thorn in the flesh' but identifies it as an aggelos, a word usually translated 'angel of Satan'. The Greek word translated 'buffet' means 'to beat to a pulp.' Under this intense pressure, Paul asked the Lord three times to take it away, and finally the Lord explained to Paul why He would not: 'My grace is sufficient for you, for my strength is made perfect in weakness.' Grace is sufficient. Grace-not human ability, not human talents, not human intellect. God's grace plus our weakness equals power in ministry."[4]

The apostle's response to God's answer to his request is a vivid example for believers of how we should deal with every thorn in our flesh. When Paul realized that his weaknesses were a conduit for the perfection of God's strength in his life, he decided to glory in his infirmities so the power of God would rest upon him. Whenever we reach a point where we think we can handle our weaknesses by ourselves, we lose power because we cannot ward off the enemy's attacks using our own strength. God's unmerited favor, His divine enablement, allows us to increase in power to the point where we can rejoice no matter what the weakness or infirmity.

The Bible never tells us to rejoice for the weakness but to rejoice *in* it. We are commanded to give thanks in everything because this is the will of the Lord. By no means is this an easy thing to do. The believer has to reach a place of maturity where she knows that the sufficiency of God's grace enables her to overcome all challenges. Paul is a great example of an individual who matured to the point where he became reliant on the Grace of God and matured in that grace to the point where he moved in the demonstration of the power of God. His life as a Pharisee and his life in Christ is a sharp contrast between legalism and grace. Prior to his Damascus Road conversion, he was not a person known for manifesting God's grace but for his strict adherence to legalism. His discourse with King Agrippa shows how the Lord transformed his life by the Damascus road encounter *(Acts 26:1–16)*.

Paul had power as a Pharisee. His power did not flow from grace, but from legalism. He thought he was using that power to do God's work, but soon found out that he was persecuting the very God he purported to serve by arresting, and imprisoning His people. How many religious and legalistic zealots are out there beating God's people over the head with the law instead of freeing them with grace? If we do not realize that our ministry for God is by grace alone *(Sola Gratia)*, then we run the risk of going forth in our own strength, which will inevitably do more harm than good to those we are trying to reach.

For God's grace to have maximum effect in our lives, we have to become totally broken before Him. We must reach the point where we are dependent on Him every waking moment. This goes against our natural tendencies because we have natural mechanisms inside us that kick in when there is danger, which prompt us to fight the battle ourselves. However, when we tap into God's grace, His power will manifest because we are letting him know that we cannot win the battle, and we will be defeated unless He intervenes. This doctrine is antithetical to what the world believes and how the world instructs us to act when faced with a crisis. The world looks at brokenness and meekness as weaknesses. Its emphasis is on self-reliance. If we examine the state of the world, we become acutely aware that man will always be a tragic figure without God's intervention. God does not break us to leave us broken; He breaks us so we can be empowered to do his will.

The Bible says we have a treasure in earthen vessels. Earthen vessels are fragile so why would God choose to put His treasure in an earthen vessel. God knows when He uses the earthen vessel, the vessel will not be able to take credit or bring attention to itself; the glory will go to God. It is a great testimony to individuals who are broken by sin to witness the difference between brokenness in God, and the brokenness that comes through sin.

"But God, who is rich in mercy, for his great love wherewith he loved us, even when we were dead in sins, hath quickened us together with Christ, (by grace ye are saved); and hath raised us up together, and made us sit together in heavenly places in Christ Jesus: That in the ages to come he might show the exceeding riches of his grace in his kindness toward us through Christ Jesus. For by grace are ye saved through faith; and that not of yourselves: it is the gift of God: Not of works, lest any man should boast" (Ephesians 2:4–9). These verses are loaded with some real golden nuggets, and I believe it is worth spending some additional time dissecting them, because they give us a marvelous insight into some of the central characteristics and attributes of God and His plan for His people.

Paul starts out by saying that God is rich in mercy, and that mercy stems from the great love that He has for us. What fascinates me about this particular verse is not the revelation of the depth of God's mercy and love (because I expect that from my God), but the object of His mercy and love. God is not like man, in that His mercy, grace, and love do not have strings attached to them. Human beings most often will manifest mercy and grace to those to whom they are connected, or people who can repay them at some point in the future; but they are not as quick to extend it to a stranger, especially if that stranger has done some reprehensible act. At that juncture, there would be a call for vengeance and retribution, not mercy and grace.

We were the recipients of God's rich mercy and great love when we were dead in our sins. God is not looking for perfect people, but people to perfect. He didn't go into palaces to find the offspring of royalty; on the contrary, He looked for the refuse and the dregs of this world. It is unfathomable to the natural mind how God can pour out such blessings upon us when we are in such a depraved state. I like to think of it in this manner: I owed God, but instead of demanding that I pay, He paid the debt for me. It is quite different in the natural. When we sell our services to an employer, we expect to be paid when the pay period comes around—We need the payment to take care of our needs. God, on the other hand, is self-sufficient and does not lack anything. He has abundance, so He is able, through Jesus, to pay all our debts. It is not done for His sake, but for ours.

Not only has He poured His mercy and love out on us when we were least deserving, but He has also quickened us together with Christ Jesus and has raised us up together, and made us sit together in heavenly places in Him. When we get a true revelation of our position in Christ, we will cease to be tormented and defeated by imps and little foxes. We are still striving to come into the fullness of our position in Christ, but we must operate from the standpoint of being raised up from a lowly place to a lofty position with Jesus. We can't afford to look at ourselves simply as sinners saved by Grace, because there is more to it than that. We must begin to look at the reason why God's wonderful grace was made available to us. The Apostle Paul does not leave us guessing, but explains the reason in Ephesians 2:7. He says, *"That in the ages to come he might show the exceeding riches of his grace in his kindness toward us through Christ Jesus."* sinners cannot do anything to earn this grace; the apostle says it comes through faith; and that not of us: it is a gift.

God made sure that man would not be able to boast or take credit for any part of salvation by supplying the faith that is necessary to receive salvation. No one can say, because I have done more work than another has, I am more deserving of salvation. God has dealt to every man the measure of faith needed for the new birth.

Unfortunately, through the ages, men have tried to gain salvation by works, but their attempts have been futile because the price of redemption is so costly it cannot be paid with anything less than the blood of God's only begotten son. The mercy seat had blood sprinkled on it on the Day of Atonement, foreshadowing the day when the blood of the lamb would be shed for those who would receive the gift that God has provided.

One of the most poignant passages of scripture that contrasts the difference between those who recognize that it is because of the unearned grace and mercy of God that we are not consumed, and those who feel like they can work their way into right standings with God, is found in Luke 18:11–13. In these particular verses, Jesus tells the parable of two men who prayed.

"And he spake this parable unto certain which trusted in themselves that they were righteous, and despised others: Two men went up into the temple to pray; the one a Pharisee, and the other a publican. The Pharisee

stood and prayed thus with himself, God, I thank thee, that I am not as other men are, extortioners, unjust, adulterers, or even as this publican. I fast twice in the week; I give tithes of all that I possess. And the publican, standing afar off, would not lift up so much as his eyes, unto heaven, but smote upon his breast, saying, God be merciful to me a sinner. I tell you, this man went down to his house justified rather than the other: for every one that exalts himself shall be abased; and he that humbles himself shall be exalted."

A) Jesus spoke the parable to religious leaders, who trusted in themselves that they were righteous and despised others. When we are deceived into trusting ourselves rather than God, we develop a false righteousness that causes us to think of ourselves more highly than we ought, and that in turn causes us to look down on others. Both men went to the temple for the same purpose, but based on how they perceived themselves, both left the temple with different results. Let's examine both men:

1) <u>The Pharisees:</u> The name Pharisee means, "Separated ones." They were one of the major religious groups in Israel at the time of Jesus. They wore special clothing to make sure everyone was impressed with who they were. They were very religious minded and were committed to obeying all facets of the Law of Moses. They were admired by the common people for their apparent piety. They believed in a bodily resurrection and eternal life; they also believed in angels and demons. They had many run-ins with Jesus because they behaved as though their own religious rules were just as important as God's rules for living. They believed salvation came from perfect obedience to the law and was not based on forgiveness of sins. Not only were they preoccupied with keeping the Mosaic Law but also the thousands of regulations added to it through the years. They loved to concern themselves with the externals, like tithing and ritual purity. They were so obsessed with obeying their legal interpretations in every detail that they completely ignored God's message of mercy and grace.

2) <u>Publicans:</u> Publicans were tax collectors who were held in contempt because they worked for the hated Romans. They were not paid by the Romans but instead received freedom in collecting taxes from their fellow Jews. Everything they could steal from the people above what was owed to the Romans was theirs. They were very shrewd when it came to siphoning funds, and that made it a lucrative business.

Notice, Jesus said that the Pharisee prayed with himself. Whenever we come before God with a self-righteous spirit, we are praying in the flesh and not praying a prayer led by the Holy Spirit. Prayers not led by the Spirit are selfish and self-righteous prayers.

Instead of going before God in repentance for his sins and asking God to deliver him, the Pharisee went to God with a list, which consisted of the persons who he was not like. He even goes as far as to thank God that he was not like the Publican, who was also there praying. After thanking God for who he was not like, he then tells God about all his self-righteous works. How different is the Pharisee's attitude to the Publican who is standing far off. Jesus said he would not even lift up his eyes to heaven, but on the contrary, he smote his breast and asked God to be merciful unto him because he was a sinner. In response to his prayer, Jesus said that the Publican, who was held in contempt by his fellow Jews, went down to his house justified rather than the Pharisee. He's justified in that he is viewed as having never committed the sin. The Pharisee returned in the same condition because he chose to exalt himself before God.

What did the Publican ask of God? He asked God to be merciful unto him. In other words, he was asking God not to deal with him according to the manner in which he deserved. He recognized his sinful and depraved state and cried out to God for mercy. Examine the names of Jesus' disciples and you will see the name of Matthew—a Publican. The man who wrote two-thirds of the New Testament and had tremendous success in the spreading of the Gospel was a converted Pharisee name Saul of Tarsus. What a wonderful example of the grace and mercy of God.

Human beings who are dead in sin and trespasses have nothing of value to offer for their lives. A sinful man cannot offer his life to God as a ransom for sin; he needs a ransom for his own sins. That is why Aaron, the high priest, had to bring blood into the most holy place for his own sins, as well as the people's sins. Jesus did not have to do that. In Hebrews 9:12, the writer states: *"Neither by the blood of goats and calves, but by his own blood he entered in once into the holy place, having obtained eternal redemption for us."*

In 2 Corinthians 5:21, the Apostle Paul writes: *"For he hath made him to be sin for us, who knew no sin; that we might be made the righteousness of God in him."* The righteousness that is spoken of is one that is imputed to us because we had no righteousness of our own. I tell you the truth: unless an individual is willing to receive the gift that God has provided for his redemption, he will not escape the wrath to come.

Men would rather enjoy the pleasures of sin for a season than to repent and call on the name of Jesus for the remission of their sins. Men would rather trample God's wonderful gift of grace by creating their own gods, who allow them to fornicate, commit adultery, and live a lascivious and licentious lifestyle. They give heed to seducing spirits sent by the adversary instead of yielding to the Holy Spirit who is calling them to repentance.

In Isaiah 59:2, the prophet wrote, *"but your iniquities have separated between you and your God, and your sins have hid his face from you, that he will not hear you."* Someone might argue that that is the Old Testament, so let me quote from the book of Romans chapter 3, verse 23: *"For all have sinned and come short of the Glory of God."* That verse simply means that we all have missed the mark, like an archer shooting to hit his target and missing it terribly. The penalty for missing that mark is death. But our merciful Father had a plan, which is found in John 3:16–17: *"for God so loved the world that He gave His only begotten Son that whosoever believeth in Him, should not perish but have eternal life."*

A songwriter wrote, *"Justice demanded that I should have died, but grace and mercy said no, I've already paid the price."* Another songwriter wrote, *"Mercy there was great and grace was free pardon there was multiplied to me; there my burdened soul found liberty at Calvary."* God did not provide salvation with a cheap grace. The price of salvation can be seen at Calvary. Humanly speaking, no one would be willing to make the type of sacrifice God made for us; But God loved us enough to sacrifice His Son for us. The ultimate sacrifice is the willingness to lay down one's life for a friend. Jesus knew the weaknesses and frailties of the disciples He chose. He knew they would abandon him at the time of His arrest; But He still called them friends and laid down His life for them. In the same manner, God knows that we mess up, and we blow it at times; but instead of wiping us out, He waits patiently for us to repent.

God not only redeemed us by sending Jesus to die in our place, He also gave us dominion. The word dominion as David, in Psalm 8, uses it is the Hebrew word *mashal*, and it means, "To rule, to reign, to have power." We have been empowered by God through faith in Jesus Christ to have power over the works of the Devil. Luke refers to this empowerment, or dominion, he wrote, *"And the seventy returned again with joy, saying, Lord, even the devils are subject unto us through thy name. And he said unto them, I beheld Satan as lightning fall from heaven. Behold, I give unto you power to tread on serpents and scorpions, and over all the power of the enemy: and nothing shall by any means hurt you."* (Luke 10:17-19).

When Jesus said *"power to tread on serpents and scorpions,"* the Greek word for power, as it is used here, is, *ex-oo-see-ah*, and it means "authority, freedom, and delegated influence." It is different from the word Jesus used when He said *"all the power of the enemy."* That power is *doo-nam-is*, and it means "miraculous power" or "the ability to work miracles." Believers love to quote the verse that says, *"one shall chase a thousand and two ten thousand."* We need to wake up and realize that with the indwelling of the Holy Spirit, we have access to all power.

The closer we get to the return of Jesus, the more lying wonders the adversary will manifest. We will face adversity because it is a part of the sanctification process in which we are being conformed to the image and likeness of Jesus. Many believers are trying to cast the Devil out of situations God has ordained for their development. My pastor, Dr. Samuel N. Greene, founder of Narrow Way Bible College says, the Sons of God will experience the dealings of God. These dealings are trials they go through that are not initiated by the Devil. He points to Job as an example of a righteous man who is afflicted at the initiation of God. This affliction was instituted to get Job to a place of greater awareness of the majesty and splendor of God. Satan was involved in Job's affliction, but only to the extent, God was the one who pointed out Job and gave the adversary permission to afflict him.

Religious people will lay a guilt trip on you to make you believe you are experiencing affliction because you are not exercising your faith. You need to go to the scriptures and search it out, and the scriptures will support the fact that God allows trials and tribulations in the life of the elect. Let us examine several scriptures that support this:

1) *Many are the afflictions of the righteous: but the Lord delivers him out of them all. The righteous will suffer many afflictions but God is the deliverer and there will be deliverance from them all" (Psalm 34:19).*
2) *"Before I was afflicted I went astray: but now have I kept thy word" (Psalm 119:67).*
3) *"It is good for me that I have been afflicted; that I might learn thy statutes" (Psalm 119:71).*

Many believers are living a defeated life, always lamenting about what the adversary is doing to them, and how he is on their backs. They talk more about the Devil than the wonderful works of God. Jesus described the Devil as the Prince of the power of the air. A prince does not have power over a king; a prince exercises the power and authority given to him by the king. Jesus is the King of Kings and the Lord of Lords. He is the conquering Lion of the Tribe of Judah. Through the promise of God to Abraham, the believer, who is the recipient of salvation, now becomes a joint heir with Jesus Christ. This means, God has made available to us that which belongs to Jesus. Jesus has all power and authority. He has sent the Holy Spirit to give us access to His power and His authority.

In Psalm 116:12, the Psalmist asked a very important question: *"what shall I render unto the Lord for all his benefits toward me?"* In verse 13, he answers the question by saying, *"I will take the cup of salvation, and call upon the name of the Lord."* There are two very important principles we must understand in the answer given by the Psalmist. The cup of salvation is the cup from which Jesus drank that provided salvation for all who would come unto him. It was not a pleasant cup because Jesus asked His Father if it was possible to take the cup. Now for the second principle found in the answer the Psalmist gave to the question, *"what shall I render unto the Lord for all his benefits toward me?"* The Lord to whom the Psalmist referred was the pre-incarnate Christ.

Jesus drank from the bitter cup, and this is why He has the power and the authority to save sinners. Many people are looking for salvation through other names like Mohammed, Buddha, and Krishna, but tell me, which one of those individuals was able to drink from the cup and shed his blood to provide a ransom for all. The Devil does not want people to know they can receive salvation and deliverance by yielding to the Lordship of Jesus.

Gene Cunningham writes, "Satan hates grace. He has reason to. Truth is the absolute standard of God's righteousness. No Man could ever attain that standard if it were not for grace. Grace is all that God can do for man because of the work of Christ on the cross. Only through grace can man have any relationship with God. What is worse, from Satan's point of view, is that grace gives all the glory to God because grace can only be received— never earned or deserved."[5]

Lucifer was an anointed Cherub who covered the throne of God and had all manner of instruments built into him. He was not satisfied with being the son of the morning and the leader of the angelic host who worshipped God. He wanted nothing less than God's Glory and desired to be the recipient of the worship due to God and God alone; that is why he attempted to exalt himself above the throne of God. He was hell bent on taking every human being with him. He knows the born again experience destines us for the glorious presence of God. We are heading to a place in God that Satan will never experience again, and he is pulling out all stops to make sure we don't get there.

Satan does not want us to give glory to God, and he will do anything within his power to keep people in darkness. Darkness brings vainglory to him. The unsaved person must realize this: If he does not apply the blood of Jesus to his life, he is under the influence of Satan, no matter how many good works he does. Faith in Jesus as Lord and savior is the only thing that can help anyone overcome the enemy.

CHAPTER 3
WANTED LIVING FAITH

"Nevertheless when the Son of man cometh, shall he find faith on the earth?" (Luke 18:8b). Thus far, we have examined mercy and grace and their importance in God's dealing with the saved and the unsaved. Now we move to faith, which is another key component in the salvation process.

The vehicle grace uses to transport God's unmerited favor or His divine enablement is faith. Jesus asked if He would find faith on the earth at His return. The question gives the connotation that Jesus will be looking for faith when he returns. Romans 12:3 says "think soberly, according as God hath dealt to every man the measure of faith." If God has given every man a measure of faith, why does Jesus' question seem to suggest that faith will be a scarce commodity when He returns. I am certain there will be men around when He returns, so is it not logical to deduce there will be faith.

To understand the type of faith Jesus will be looking for, we must make a distinction between the type of faith that allows us to go into a building and not worry that it will collapse, and the type of faith expressed when the elect cry day and night unto him. We don't please God because we have a measure of faith. When He is not the object of the measure, the measure becomes an ordinary thing we use to get through life. The faith He will be looking for is a vibrant, active faith that has God at its center. "For we walk by faith, not by sight" (2 Corinthians 5:7). This verse does not ask us if we walk by faith, and it does not tell us to walk by faith. The apostle's assumption is that the believer is walking by faith. The term carnal Christian sounds like an oxymoron, but many believers are operating based on how they see things in the

33

natural. The adversary is a master illusionist and counterfeiter. He is able to manipulate those believers who walk by sight. God is not saying we should walk around with our heads in the clouds, oblivious to natural occurrences.

The type of faith that pleases God, and the faith Jesus will be looking for, is the faith that trusts God to make a way when there seems to be no way. Never deal with life's challenges through carnal means, no matter how effective they may seem. Hebrews 11 is called the hall of faith because it contains the story of several individuals who put their faith and trust in God while facing formidable odds. It gives us a vivid picture of what faith is and why it pleases God.

Hebrews 11:1 "Now faith is the substance of things hoped for, the evidence of things not seen."

A) Substance: (hoop-os-tas-is) A setting under, support. It is a compound word. Hoop-o: Under or beneath His-tay-mee: covenant, establish, to hold up

Our faith in Christ is not based on some pie in the sky notion, some philosophical fancy, or some flimsy evidence: We are under-girded by a sure foundation. We are standing on a covenant written in the blood of Jesus, so the unseen things, which are promised to us by God, will be accessed by our faith because our faith is tangible. Faith itself is the evidence of the things for which we are hoping. When the writer uses the word hope, he does not mean a wish. In the Greek, it is *el-pid-zo*, and it means, "To expect or confide." It comes from the root *elpis*, which means, "to anticipate, usually with pleasure, expectation, or confidence."

Worldly hope is uncertain and leaves an individual feeling nervous. They do not have a blessed assurance that the object hoped for will manifest. It is sort of a hit or miss—maybe it will come to pass or maybe it will not. Uncertainty should never be the disposition of a child of Jesus Christ. God's children must have a firm expectation that He will perform what He has promised. The believer's anticipation is with pleasure, not doubt. If we doubt, we are not expressing the God kind of faith, or the hope that springs from pleasurable expectation. Worry and fear have no place in the mind of the believer that places her trust in God, and believes in Him for breakthroughs and deliverance.

Are you facing a medical, marital, or financial crisis? Just trust

God, and remember that faith and fear are diametrically opposed to each other. The Apostle Paul told his son Timothy that, *"God has not given us a spirit of fear, but of power, and of love, and of a sound mind" (2 Timothy 1:7)*. Remember, power in the Greek is *doo-nam-is*, and it means, "Miraculous power, abundance, and force."

Hebrew 11:2: *"For by it the elders obtained a good report."* The elders are seasoned individuals who have been purified in the furnace of affliction, and have come out with a testimony concerning the faithfulness of God. They obtained a good report because their faith in God was not weakened by the tribulations they experienced. On the contrary, their faith was strengthened by it.

Hebrews 11:3: *"Through faith we understand that the worlds were framed by the word of God, so that things which are seen were not made of things which do appear."* Physicists have their theories of how the world came into existence, whether it is the big bang or some other theory. If they would take the time to meditate on *Hebrews 11:3*, they would save themselves a great deal of time and money. *Psalm 14:1a* states, *"The fool hath said in his heart, there is no God."* Many scientists would rather believe some theory for the earth's existence in order to factor God out of the creation equation. *"But God hath chosen the foolish things of the world to confound the wise; and God hath chosen the weak things of the world to confound the things which are mighty" (1 Corinthians 1:27)*. The word of God can transform the life of a man or woman dwelling in a hut in some distant rain forest. Without a formal education, they can come to an understanding of the creation of the world by God through His word. The scientist who has more degrees than a Thermometer will struggle to understand how the worlds were framed because he or she rejects the existence of God.

The Holy Spirit revealed to me that when the writer says, "things which are seen were not made by things which do appear," He is referring to reality and greater reality. Therefore, the reality of what we see in the natural is superseded by the greater reality of the unseen God who made them. The point I am expressing is this: the thing that is created can never be greater than He who created it, because everything He created, He created with His word. We should never be intimated by what we see because our faith in the one who is unseen is greater. This is the reason why the Apostle Paul said, *"walk by faith and not by sight."* Cancer is a reality, but the healing power of Jesus is a greater reality. Terrorism is a reality, but the fact that light has triumphed over darkness is a greater reality. False religion is a reality, but the fact that Jesus is the way, the truth, and the life is the greater reality.

1 John 4:4: "Ye are of God, little children, and have overcome them: because greater is he that is in you, than he that is in the world." Who is the greater one that is in us? He is the word that became flesh and first dwelt among us, and through the power of the Holy Spirit He now dwells in us. He is the one spoken of in John 1:1, *"In the beginning was the Word, and the Word was with God, and the Word was God. The same was in the beginning with God. All things were made by him; and without him was not any thing made that was made."* The things that do appear were made from things that are unseen. The unseen one, the Logos, according to John, is the one who created it all. He has come to tabernacle with us, so if He is now in us, and He is the greater reality, how can we allow the reality of any situation to strike fear in us? Whose report will you believe? When you get this revelation, you will understand why we must trust in Him and nothing else—why we must declare His Lordship over everything that is seen and unseen.

When we get this revelation, we will understand what the Apostle Paul meant when he quoted Habakkuk 2:4 *"the just shall live by his faith."* The just shall live by the measure of faith God has given him. The person who is justified by Jesus Christ will live according to the measure of faith he or she activates. You do not need a whole lot of faith; you need to act upon the measure you have received. *"but what saith it? The word is nigh thee, even in thy mouth, and in thy heart: that is, the word of faith, which we preach."* *(Romans 10:8).* The word that comes out of our mouth should be the word of faith. *"For out of the abundance of the heart the mouth speaketh" (Matthew 12:34b).* If the heart is full of doubt and fear, the mouth will speak doubt and fear. Have you ever spent time around believers that are always speaking negative? No matter how you encourage them to trust God, and stand on his word, they seem to place the word "but" before every sentence. Pray for them, and do not allow the negative spirit to operate around you. The faith-filled believer does not face challenges with doubt.

When we encounter a difficult situation, we must be careful how we speak. Do not speak doubt because doubt is to the adversary what faith is to God. God has placed the word of faith in our mouth so we can launch it like a guided missile against the enemy. There is power and authority in the word and faith gives us confidence that God will back up His word.

Words can construct or destruct; the Bible says, *"Death and life are in the power of the tongue: and they that love it shall eat the fruit thereof"* (Proverbs 18:21).The person who coined the phrase, "sticks and stones may break my bones but words will never hurt me," was lying. Sometimes words can cause more harm than sticks and stones.

Dr. R. C. Sproul gives us some great insight into the majesty of God and His creative Word. He writes, "I sat in terrified silence the first day of my freshman class in astronomy. The professor posed a question for us: "Suppose that we have a scale wherein an inch equals a million miles. How far would it be to the nearest star apart from our sun? Would it be one hundred feet? Three hundred feet? Or five hundred feet?"

My mind began to calculate frantically. Twelve inches equals one foot. One foot then would mean twelve million miles. Multiply that by one hundred, and the first option meant a distance of over a billion miles. Now, I knew that our sun was ninety-three million miles from the earth. It seemed reasonable that the next nearest star would not be much more than ten times that distance, so I guessed one hundred feet was the correct answer. I was wrong. So were all the other students who guessed either three hundred feet or five hundred feet. The professor fooled us. "He said, none of the above." He went on to explain that the nearest star was approximately the distance from Pittsburgh to Chicago, with each inch equaling a million miles. He gave us a little more help.

"Light travels at a rate of 186,000 miles per second," he said. "That is, in one second light can travel seven-and-a-half times around the earth. The light that we see twinkling at night from the nearest star left that star on its way to Earth four-and-a-half years ago!" The distance from earth to the nearest star is four-and-a-half light years away. Traveling at a speed of 186,000 miles per second it takes over four years to reach us! I could not fathom such immensity.

When I left class, I was in a daze. I had mixed feelings. On the one hand, I was staggered by the apparent insignificance of planet Earth and of R.C. Sproul. I felt like a speck in a vast universe. Yet, I was also awestruck by the sheer magnitude of power that could make a universe so gigantic as to contain billions of stars that were mega billions of distances from each other. My mind snapped back to Genesis. *"In the beginning, God created the heavens and the earth. The earth was without form, and void; and darkness was on the face of the deep. And the Spirit of God was hovering over the face of the waters. Then God said, 'Let there be light'; and there was light"* (Genesis 1:1–3). The last line—"and there was light"—is totally mystifying! God spoke. He commanded light to come into existence. Light began to shine. This is what Saint Augustine called the Divine Imperative. The world was created by the sheer power of God's voice.[6]

God is the only one who can create *ex-nehilo*. This means God can create something out of nothing. Man has the ability to take material that is already present and fashion that material into something else. God is unique in that He does not have to use anything to fashion something new. God can make the immaterial material. If you find yourself in a situation that appears to be void of substance, don't panic. Draw on that creative word that is in you and allow the word of faith to create something substantive. Remember, the word of faith in you is an actual substance of the things you are hoping for, and the evidence of that which is unseen. With the word of God you can make the unseen seen.

The Ek-zay-te-o Factor

Now we look at the verse I consider the heart of Hebrews 11. Verse 6 states, *"But without faith it is impossible to please Him: for he that comes to God must believe that He is, and that he is a rewarder of them that diligently seek him."* In verse six, the writer sums up the importance of faith by telling us that it is impossible to please God without it. If I had never read verse six and someone came to me and asked what I needed to do to please God, I probably would not mention faith as my first response. Most likely, I would mention some deed, like, not lying, stealing, or committing adultery, because the natural tendency is to think of some type of work.

Everything in our relationship with God is predicated upon our faith in Him; if we don't believe in Him then obviously we will not endeavor to know Him. Again, I want to exegete and delve deeper into the word of God.

As important as our Belief in God is, it is not an end in itself but a means to an end. Belief introduces us to Him, but intimacy is not gained just because one is introduced to Him. My argument that belief is the beginning and not the end is backed up by the Apostle James. In 2:19, he writes, *"Thou believest that there is one God; thou doest well: the devils also believe, and tremble."* James said the devils believe and tremble, so we must go beyond mere belief. There are people who believe there is a God, but that belief does not lead them to a deeper commitment to Him. When James uses the word belief, he is using the Greek word *pist-yoo-o*; it is from the root *pis-tis,* and it means "truth," or "the truthfulness of God or a religious teacher." James is not saying there is any truth in the devils because they believe; what he is saying is the devils know the truthfulness of who God is, so the born again believer must not rest on their belief. They must press on to know Him intimately. This pressing on to know Him intimately is explained in verse 6. The writer states, *"He that comes to God must believe that He is, and that He is a rewarder of them that diligently seek Him."*

Before I expound on the word diligent, please allow me the courtesy of dispelling any thought that there can be any smattering of works by man, which aid in the salvation process. Jesus is the savior; grace, mercy, and faith are the tools He uses. Man can take no credit for salvation; he is totally at the mercy of Jesus. In chapter four in his treatise on justification by faith, Paul asked the question, *"For what saith the scripture? Abraham believed God, and it was counted unto him for righteousness."* He was not discounting the fact that we are called to be co-laborers with Christ. He is letting the reader know that as far as the salvation process goes, it is strictly by faith alone (*Sola Fide*). After all, the Apostle Paul was one of the most consistent laborers for Christ.

He identifies Abraham as an example for us of a man who received righteousness because he believed God. The type of works the apostle assails in his writings on justification by faith is the self-centered type which man does so he can take some credit for salvation.

F.F. Bruce, the former Emeritus Professor at the University

of Manchester, expounded on Abraham's justification by faith when he wrote, "Abraham's justification and attendant blessings were based on his faith in God; they were not earned by merit or effort on his part (as would have been the case had they been conditional on law-keeping) but conferred on him by God's grace. And the principle on which God thus dealt with Abraham extends to his descendants—not to his natural descendants as such, for they have become subject to the obligations of the law, but to his spiritual descendants, those who follow the precedent of Abraham's faith. This, says Paul, is what God meant when he gave him the name Abraham (in place of Abram, as he was formerly called), and said, *'I have made you the father of a multitude of nations'* (Genesis 17:5). These comprise all who believe in God, Jews and Gentiles alike: Abraham is the father of all believers."[7] I make no apologies for hammering out the fact that it dishonors God when men try to attach works to faith in the salvation equation. I take the time and diligence to do this because I want to avoid any ambiguities when I defend the centrality of my argument. The argument is that true faith in God energizes the faithful to labor, not for salvation, because that comes through faith, but for the establishment of the Kingdom of God in the hearts and minds of people.

Bruce goes on to say, "Consider, too, the quality of Abraham's faith. It was faith in the God who brings the dead to life, who calls non-existent things as though they really existed— and gives them real existence by doing so. When God told him that he would have a vast multitude of descendents, Abraham was still childless. Not only so, but he was beyond the age at which a man might reasonably hope to become a father, and Sarah his wife was even more certainly beyond the age of motherhood. Abraham did not shut his eyes to these unfavorable circumstances; he took them all into careful consideration. But, when he set over against them the promise of God, he found that the certainty of God's ability and will to fulfill his promise outweighed the all. Having nothing to rest upon but the bare word of God, he relied on that, in face of all the opposing indications that pressed on him from every side. In fact, the very force of the obstacles that lay in its path strengthened his faith. And his faith won him the favor of God."[8]

Abraham refused to allow the deadness of his body and

Sarah's womb to affect the word that came from God. He was diligent in his belief in God's word. His diligence produced an abundance of blessings, not only for himself but also for all the families of the earth.

The word diligent in the Greek is, *Ek-zay-te-o*, which means "to seek out, to search for, to crave, to demand." Now we begin to understand why the believer has to move from the place of mere belief. God wants us to demand an audience with Him; He wants us to pursue Him with a passion. He wants us to crave His presence as a man dying of thirst craves a drink of cool spring water. *Ek-zay-te-o* means I do whatever is necessary in the Holy Ghost to receive an audience with Jesus. The purpose of my passionate pursuit is not material things. The ultimate purpose is to bask in His glorious presence, because in His presence, there is fullness of joy.

The adversary throws all kinds of roadblocks in our way. His intention is to hinder us from God's presence. We must be single-minded and determined in our pursuit of Him. This type of pursuit, craving, or searching is not for the faint of heart. It is not for the religious minded who have a form of godliness but deny His power. This pursuit is for radical believers whose primary focus is God. In *Psalm 42:1*, David wrote, *"As the hart panteth after the water brooks, so panteth my soul after thee, O God."* The word pant in the Hebrew is *aw-rag*, and it means "to long for—to cry." The soul is the seat of the intellect, the will, and the emotions. It is the place where we make decisions, the place where we feel. David is saying that his mind, his emotions, and his will crave and cries out for God. In *Psalm 34:8*, he says, *"my soul shall make her boast in the Lord: the humble shall hear thereof, and be glad."* Religious devils and the enemies of worship are always trying to silence the praises of God's people. They criticize worshippers who shout unto God with the voice of triumph. They need to know that we are not shouting to be seen, we are shouting because our shout is like a cannon blast in the atmosphere, which routs principalities and powers. Those who are humble in the sight of the Lord are glad when we boast in Him.

Beloved, it is important for us to study deeply the word God has provided for us. We should be careful not to approach the word with a cavalier attitude, as if it is just another book on our shelf. A deeper study of belief, faith, and diligently, shows us what pleases God. They also show us how we should pursue him. In *Psalm 34:1*, David wrote, *"I will bless the LORD at all times: his praise shall continually be in my mouth."* The word praise, as David uses it, is the Hebrew word *the-hil-aw*, and it comes from the word *haw-lal.* The word *haw-lal* means "to shine, to make a show, to boast; and thus to be (clamorously) foolish; to rave to celebrate; also to stultify." According to Random House Webster's Collegiate Dictionary, the word *stultify* means, "to make, or cause to appear, foolish or ridiculous."

True faith does not find its expression in seeking God for things. True faith continually seeks out God to bestow upon Him the praise, honor, and glory due to His Holy name. Religion desires to stifle true faith because religion's motivation is maintaining control. When we are seeking God like the deer panting for the water brook, it does not matter to us what we look or sound like to others. We lose all self-righteousness and false pride, and like the elders in Revelation 24, we throw down our crowns of human accomplishment and worship the Lamb of God. True faith defies the spirit of Michal, which uses the stare of intimidation and the words of accusation to criticize the men and women of God who realize they were created to worship King Jesus.

"And as the ark of the LORD came into the city of David, Michael Saul's daughter looked through a window, and saw King David leaping and dancing before the LORD; and she despised him in her heart" (2 Samuel 6:16). Believers who understand the importance of the *Ek-zay-te-o* factor always find themselves being criticized, and ostracized, by the hidden agenda of religion. We must respond in the same manner King David responded to Michal when she said, *"How glorious was the king of Israel to day, who uncovered himself to day in the eyes of the handmaids of his servants, as one of the vain fellows shamelessly uncovers himself!"* (2 Samuel 16:20b).

David's response was, *"It was before the LORD, which chose me before thy father, and before his entire house, to appoint me ruler over the people of the LORD, over Israel: therefore will I play before the LORD. And I will yet be more vile than thus, and will be base in mine own sight"* (2 Samuel 6:22a). The leaders of God's people who He has put in charge as stewards cannot be arrogant and puffed up; they must always be an example of what it means to seek after God with radical worship.

The Gospel writer Mark recorded the story of a woman who went beyond mere belief. She tapped into the *Ek-zay-te-o* factor in order to get a healing for her demon-possessed daughter. Her story is told in Mark 7:24–30. Jesus appears to be in a house enjoying some quiet time with his disciples. The writer says Jesus did not want any man to know where He was. A woman with a craving, a woman who would not be denied an audience with Him, interrupted the quiet time. Jesus could not be hid because true faith is like a heat-seeking missile that finds the warmth of His compassion and love for those in dire need.

She is not from Israel because Mark describes her as a Greek, a Syrophenician by nation. We are not told how she found out Jesus was in the house, but she must have done some serious detective work because Jesus did not want anyone to know He was there. Through her intelligence network, she heard of Him, and came and fell at His feet, desiring that He would cast the unclean spirit out of her daughter.

When I first read this account by Mark as a young Christian, I was very perplexed by Jesus' response to her request. Jesus told her the children should be filled first: because it was not meet to take the children's bread, and to cast it to the dogs. It seemed offensive to me that Jesus would call her a dog, so I asked my wife, who was more mature in the Lord than I was at the time. She explained that the woman's faith was being tested by Jesus. Remember that at the outset we established the fact that belief was the means and not the end. The reward does not go to the casual believer but to the diligent, the ones who understand the *Ek-zay-te-o* factor.

Jesus had come for the lost sheep of Israel, and the gentiles were considered dogs. The woman's response is a shining example of why we should be abased in our own eyes when we are in the presence of the King. Many people would have walked away with an attitude because of the hard saying, but she said to Jesus, *"Yes, Lord: yet the dogs under the table eat of the children's crumbs."* She agreed with Him because she knew that He spoke the truth. She told Him that the crumbs from the children's bread that fell from the table were feeding the natural dogs, so surely He could spare a crumb for her child. Her act of faith produced the healing her daughter needed.

Many believers have reduced faith to naming it and claiming

it, blabbing it and grabbing it. Many believes are settling for the crumbs that are falling off the table of religion, but God is perfecting Himself in a remnant who are looking to the Bread of Heaven for their sustenance, and they will not settle for the stale bread offered to them through false doctrine. They recognize their position as sons and daughters, children of the most High God, and joint heirs with Jesus. The do not base their faith on vain materialism but on a sincere desire to see people, who are living like rabid dogs, come into an intimate relationship with the Lord Jesus. In the Parable of the unjust judge, Jesus said, *"nevertheless when the Son of man cometh, shall he find faith on the earth"* (Luke 18:8b)? My answer to this question is a resounding yes, but He will not find much of it in organized religion. He will find it amongst the remnant that cry day and night, though He bear long with them. It will be a remnant that has overcome the adversary by the blood of the Lamb and the word of their testimony.

CHAPTER 4
THE BLOOD OF JESUS CHRIST: THE LAMB OF GOD

For the life of the flesh is in the blood: and I have given it to you upon the altar to make an atonement for your souls: for it is the blood that maketh an atonement for the soul" (Leviticus 17:11). It was the morning of September 11, 2001, and I was at the daycare of the church I attended. The memory is so vivid it might as well be yesterday. The daycare director called my attention to the news flash coming from the television. The news anchor was reporting that a plane had just crashed into the World Trade Center. I watched in horror as flames engulfed the towers. While trying to come to terms with the tragic events unfolding, another plane flew into the other tower. I knew immediately that the nation was under attack and life as I knew it had changed forever.

While watching the horrific scene unfold, I received a call from my sister Nena. She informed me that our sister Janet worked in one of the towers. At that very moment, the tragedy hit home and became more personal than ever. There is a tendency to become desensitized and detached because of all the murder and mayhem we watch and listen to on the evening news. We see graphic images of people being blown up and gunned down. We feel a sense of remorse but also a sense of detachment when we do not know the victim or victims. When the victim is a loved one, words cannot describe the utter distress and helplessness that is felt, but words will have to suffice.

Once I found out that my sister might be in one of the buildings, I left the daycare immediately and headed home. I remember praying to the Lord for mercy, not only for Janet but also for every other person in the building and for the many families affected by the tragedy.

45

That afternoon, I received word that Janet had made it out of the towering inferno, and I was grateful yet saddened by the great loss of other families. When I spoke with Janet, she told me she felt the building shake and saw a crack in the wall and knew she was in danger. She explained that she fled the building, and when she made it outside, she found the area blanketed by a thick cloud of ash, which made breathing difficult, and at one point sought refuge under an ambulance. The atmosphere was so thick with the ash that Janet could not see. She heard a voice while she was under the ambulance, saying, "Open the door and let people in." Thinking the ambulance was about to pull off with her under it, she reached out and was pulled inside. She told me the thing that kept her going was a message she remembered ministering called the Blood of Jesus. She kept saying, "The Blood of Jesus, The Blood of Jesus, The Blood of Jesus."

Mercy and Grace allows us to escape divine judgment in order to receive salvation. Faith is the vehicle that carries us to salvation. Now we come to the cleansing agent used by God to cleanse us of our sins to facilitate salvation. This agent is the Blood of Jesus Christ, the Lamb of God. One of the first things a doctor will do to determine what is ailing a sick individual is to order blood work. Blood work not only identifies what is attacking our system but also helps the doctor to rule out other illnesses. God said He has given us the blood to make atonement for our souls: For it is the blood that makes atonement for the soul. The Hebrew word for atonement is *Kaw-far* and it means "to cover, to expiate, or to cancel." It also means "to cleanse, to disannul, or to be merciful." I like the definition that was given to me by one of my Bible professors and mentor, Dr. Lillian Ferguson. Dr. Ferguson said, "Atonement is when two individuals or entities that have been separated are brought back together as one."

We have already established the fact that the soul is the seat of the human will, intellect, and emotion. Let us go deeper into this concept. Genesis 2:7 states, *"And the Lord God formed man of the dust of the ground, and breathed into his nostrils the breath of life; and man became a living soul."* The Hebrew word for soul is *Neh-fesh*, and it means, "To breathe, to be breathed upon, or refreshed (as if by a current of air)." God breathed the breath of life into man, and he in turn began to breathe, think, and to feel. Meditate for a moment on the fact that blood carries the air we breathe throughout the body so life can be sustained. If an individual's blood is contaminated, the contamination is carried throughout the body by the blood.

Something happened to cause a breach in the relationship between man and the God who breathed the breath of life into him. That something made an altar of sacrifice necessary for atonement. A three-letter word encapsulates the cause of the breach. The word is sin. The word sin in the Greek is *ham-ar-tee-ah*, and it means "offence." It comes from the root *ham-ar-tan-o*, which means, "to miss the mark (and so not share in the prize)." Beloved, the prize is the high calling spoken of by the Apostle Paul in *Philippians 3:14*. It is the entrance into the presence of God to hear Him say, *"Well done, thou good and faithful servant: thou hast been faithful over a few things, I will make thee ruler over many things: enter thou into the joy of thy Lord"* (Matthew 25:23).

Think about an archer trying to hit a bull's-eye, yet constantly missing the mark. Where does the sin come from that is so evident in the world? Judaism and Islam do not believe that man is born in sin. Is man sinful because there is sin in the world or is there sin in the world because sinful man is in the world? It is interesting to note that no matter where you find men, no matter what his age, race, gender, or socioeconomic background, you will find sin wherever he is. If man does not have a sinful nature then why do we have to teach children how to do good, and not evil? Someone might say children learn evil in the world, but before a child is exposed to the world, we find ourselves struggling to teach him right from wrong. All human beings are genetically predisposed to certain things because of their parents and their parent's parents. Many people are born with genes that make them susceptible to certain diseases, so why then is it inconceivable that we can be predisposed to sin because of our progenitor? Let us examine what the scripture says by taking a trip down the Roman Road.

In Romans 3:23, the Apostle Paul writes, *"All have sinned and come short of the glory of God."* As far as I know, all still means everyone. The word glory in the Greek is *dox-ah*, and it means "dignity, honor, praise, and worship." Worship means to ascribe worth and value to God. Sin deadens and perverts our spiritual sensitivity so we are unable to see God in His splendor and majesty. Because of sin, we view Him as the cosmic bully out to execute a warrant for our arrest. Sin forces man to make a futile attempt to flee the Omnipresence of God.

Dr. Sproul writes, "For those who have tasted the sweetness of the forgiveness of and reconciliation with God, His ubiquity is good news. But for those who remain hostile and estranged from God, His omnipresence is very bad news. There is nothing a fugitive wants to hear less than that his pursuer is everywhere. There is no place to hide from an infinite spirit. His eye is on the sparrow when it falls. His eye is also on the thief when he steals. There are those who hate God's presence because they cannot stand His gaze. But for those who love His appearing, the presence of God is like soothing music."[9]

After telling the reader that all human beings have sinned and come short of God's glory, the Apostle then tells the reader the result of sin and the gift God has provided. In Romans 6:23, he writes, *"the wages of sin is death: but the gift of God is eternal life through Jesus Christ our Lord."* Before we examine the gift, its relation to the blood sacrifice, and how God has provided it, let us examine the origin of sin and how it has affected all human beings.

The book of Genesis is a book of beginnings. In the book, we find the description of the beginning of the earth, the creation of man and woman, and their placement in a beautiful garden by God. Gen 2:15–17 states, *"And the LORD God took the man, and put him into the Garden of Eden to dress it and to keep it. And the LORD God commanded the man, saying, Of every tree of the garden thou mayest freely eat: But of the tree of the knowledge of good and evil, thou shalt not eat of it: for in the day that thou eatest thereof thou shalt surely die."*

It is worth noting that the knowledge of evil is in the garden with the knowledge of good. The reader might ask why the knowledge of evil was in the garden with the knowledge of good. The author's answer is that it is there for God's divine purpose, and that purpose will be revealed to us when we meet God. Isaiah 45:5–7 states, *"I am the LORD, and there is none else, there is no God beside me: I girded thee, though thou hast not known me: That they may know from the rising of the sun, and from the west, that there is none beside me. I am the LORD, and there is none else. I form the light, and create darkness: I make peace, and create evil: I the LORD do all these things."* Was the knowledge of evil in the garden to test the free will God had given to Adam? That is a possibility. At a point of time unknown to us, that free will was tested, and the result led to catastrophic consequences. Genesis 3:1 states, *"Now the serpent was more subtle than any beast of the field which the Lord God had made. And he said unto the woman, yea, has God said, you shall not eat of every tree of the garden?"*

The word subtle in the Hebrew is *aw-room*, and it means "cunning (usually in a bad way), or crafty." The serpent probes the woman to discern her knowledge of the commandment of the Lord. A probe is sent to gather information in order to determine the best way to attack. The serpent was looking for an opening, and the woman's response provided one. It is important to point out that the creature that conversed with the woman did not look like a snake at that point, although it had the subtlety and the craftiness of one. Gene Cunningham writes, "The Hebrew word for serpent is *nachash*, and it means 'the shining one.' Not until after the fall did God curse the serpent and it became a symbol of sin. In Revelation 12:9 the serpent is identified as the devil, Satan, the one who deceives the world."[10]

Genesis 3:2–3 gives us Eve's response: *"And the woman said unto the serpent, we may eat of the fruit of the trees of the garden: But of the fruit of the tree which is in the midst of the garden, God has said, you shall not eat of it, neither shall you touch I, lest you die."*

To her credit, the woman attempts to defend the word of God but unfortunately she misquotes him. God did not tell them they could not touch the fruit. He told them they could not eat it. Ignorance of God's word was the opening the adversary was looking for, and he wasted no time in attacking that weakness. When he first comes to the woman he is asking a question, but once he gets his answer he makes an emphatic statement. Genesis 3:4-5: *"And the serpent said unto the woman, you shall not surely die: For God does know that in the day you eat thereof, then your eyes shall be opened, and you shall be as gods, knowing good and evil" (Genesis 3:4-5)*. He entices the woman with a partial truth. Her eyes would be open once she ate of the tree, but the serpent did not tell her what she would see. He led her to believe that she would be like God.

There is nothing wrong with wanting to be like God in terms of having Godly characteristics, but the serpent's idea of being like God is actually a perverted desire to receive the honor and worship due to God alone. Isaiah backs up this assertion, in chapter 14:12–16. The prophet wrote, *"How art thou fallen from heaven, O Lucifer, son of the morning! How art thou cut down to the ground, which didst weaken the nations! For thou hast said in thine heart, I will ascend into heaven, I will exalt my throne above the stars of God: I will sit also upon the mount of the congregation, in the sides of the north: I will ascend above the heights of the clouds; I will be like the most High. Yet thou shalt be brought down to hell, to the sides of the pit. They that see thee shall narrowly look upon thee, and consider thee, saying, Is this the man that made the earth to tremble, that did shake kingdoms; That made the world as a wilderness, and destroyed the cities thereof; that opened not the house of his prisoners?"*

He knew first hand the result of rebelling against God's word. Cunningham writes, "He knows that Eve is thinking in terms of physical death. He also knows that she will not fall down and die physically the instant she eats from the tree, so his words are half-true. God's warning in Genesis 2:17 uses the Hebrew word for death, muth, twice: 'In the day you eat of this tree, dying you shall surely die.' God was telling them that they would eventually die physically."[11]

The question one has to ask is this: How can we become like God by disobeying God? Adam and Eve found out the answer to that question. Genesis 3:6–7: *"And when the woman saw that the tree was good for food, and that it was pleasant to the eyes, and a tree to be desired to make one wise, she took of the fruit thereof, and did eat, and gave also unto her husband with her; and he did eat. And the eyes of them both were opened, and they knew that they were naked; and they sewed fig leaves together, and made themselves aprons."*

It is a sad indictment on Adam that he did not intervene when the serpent was conversing with his wife. He was placed in the garden to have dominion and at a crucial moment, he was missing in action. There are many men who are missing in spiritual action, and their homes are left uncovered. When Adam appears, he is disobeying the commandment of God and transferring dominion of the world to the devil. The Bible says they hear the voice of the Lord God walking in the garden in the cool of the day: and Adam and his wife hid themselves from the presence of the Lord God amongst the trees of the garden. I guess they figured that since they had fig leaves on, they could blend in with the trees. When God confronts him with the rhetorical question, "Adam where art thou?" he explains to God that he heard His voice, in the garden, and was afraid, because he was naked, so he hid himself. Sinners have been attempting to hide from God ever since. When tragedy strikes the first thing they ask is, "Why did God allow it to happen?"

God is omniscient, so He is not ignorant of their location. He is giving Adam a chance to confess and acknowledge his condition before Him. Instead of confessing his sin and falling on the mercies of God, Adam and Eve play what I call the blame game. When God asked him who told him that he was naked, and whether he'd eaten from the forbidden tree, Adam tells God, *"The woman whom thou gavest to be with me, she gave me of the tree, and I did eat" (Genesis 3:12).* He was speaking the truth, but he neglected to mention the fact that he had dropped the ball by not protecting his wife from the serpent. It is ironic that when he first saw Eve, his response was, *"this is now bone of my bones, and flesh of my flesh" (Genesis 2:23).* When tragedy strikes, she is the woman God gave to him. He does not mention the fact that He had dominion and should have protected her from the deceptive serpent. When Eve is confronted, she says, *"the serpent beguiled me, and I did eat"* (Genesis 3:13). She spoke the truth also, but God did not ask her what the serpent did, He asked her what *she* did.

Their attempt to cover themselves with an apron made of fig leaves is man's first attempt to expiate his sin through a covering. Today we see men and women trying to cover their nakedness with everything but what God has provided. From very early on, God showed us that the shedding of blood would be the method used to cleanse mankind of sin. He also tells us who would provide the blood. Gen. 3:21 says, *"Unto Adam also and to his wife did the LORD God make coats of skins, and clothed them."* In *Genesis 3:15*, we have what is called the *proto evangel.* The *proto evangel* is the first mention of God's plan to defeat the enemy through the seed of the woman and bring forth restoration. In speaking to the serpent, God said, *"And I will put enmity between thee and the woman, and between thy seed and her seed; it shall bruise thy head, and thou shalt bruise his heel."* From this passage, we understand that the deliverer would come from the seed of a woman. God is truly a God of restoration. Sin entered the world because she was deceived, but God would bring forth the promised seed through a woman.

The calling of Abram by God is a watershed event in the Bible in preparation for the promised seed. God called him from the land of Ur of the Chaldees. Abram was seventy-five when the

Lord called him; his wife Sarai was sixty-five. Abram's obedience to the call of God is astounding when you consider the fact that God asked him to leave all that was familiar to go to a land that He would show him. His obedience is the primary reason he is called the father of the faithful. If a seventy-five-year-old man and his sixty-five-year-old wife can do it, no one has an excuse.

God promised him that he would have a son. In an attempt to expedite the process, Sarai convinced Abram to sleep with her maid Hagar. Hagar bears him a son, whom he named Ishmael. The Lord next appears to Abram when he is ninety years old and promises to make a covenant with him. It is at this time that the Lord changes his name to Abraham. The name Abraham means father of many nations, and is symbolic of the promise from God to make his descendants innumerable like the sand on the seashore. His wife's name was changed to Sarah, which means mother of nations. Sarah conceived and bore Abraham a son when he was a hundred years old, and he named him Isaac.

At a certain point in time, Abraham is given the test of a lifetime by God. *"And it came to pass after these things, that God did tempt Abraham, and said unto him, Abraham: and he said, Behold, here I am. And he said, Take now thy son, thine only son Isaac, whom thou lovest, and get thee into the land of Moriah; and offer him there for a burnt offering upon one of the mountains which I will tell thee of"* (Gen 22:1–2).

When they arrive at Mount Moriah, Isaac asked his dad where the sacrifice was. Abram's answer paints a portrait for us of how to trust God. He told Isaac, *"God will provide himself a lamb for a burnt offering"* (Genesis 22:8a). I like to interpret this as, God the Son would offer himself as the Paschal Lamb.

The word tempt in Hebrew is not used in the same way as we use it in English. The Hebrew word for tempt is *naw-saw*, and it means, "to test, or to prove." In this particular verse, Abraham is a type of the father willing to sacrifice his beloved son. The word type means, *a class, group, or category of things or persons sharing one or more characteristics.* Isaac is a type of the savior because he is a promised seed. Abraham saw Mount Moriah on the third day. Three is a number that represents resurrection and increase. The Savior would be the way, the truth, and the life, He would be crucified the third hour, but He would rise on the third day. The word *Moriah* means, "Chosen by God," and it represents a place and time when God will call upon every individual. The purpose of the call will be to test us to determine if there is anything in our lives so dear that we are unwilling to lay it on the altar of sacrifice. The time and the place of that sacrifice will not be one of convenience for us, but for God. Abraham called the name of the place Jehovah Jireh, which means, "The Lord will provide." I like to give it the definition, "the provision of the Lord will be seen."

Abraham's willingness to obey the command of God to sacrifice his beloved son Isaac elicits a powerful response from God. Because of his willingness and his obedience, the Lord said to him, *"in blessing I will bless you, and in multiplying I will multiply your seed as the stars of the heaven and as the sand which is upon the sea shore; and thy seed shall possess the gate of his enemies. In thy seed shall all the nations of the earth be blessed; because thou hast obeyed my voice" (Genesis 22:17-18).* Beloved, no matter what the situation or circumstance we may face, let us endeavor to obey the still small voice of God. Inherent in His still small voice is the blessing we need to give us peace, comfort, and deliverance from our troubles.

Isaac eventually has two sons named Esau and Jacob. Jacob had twelve sons, and one of them, named Joseph, was sold into slavery by his brothers. Joseph winds up in Egypt, and after many trials, he is elevated to second in command. While Joseph is in Egypt, there is a famine in the land and his father sends all his brothers to buy corn except the youngest. Joseph eventually reveals himself to his brothers but alleviates their fear of retribution by telling them that God sent him before them to preserve posterity in the earth, and to save their lives by a great deliverance. Joseph's family eventually moves to Egypt and begins to prosper and multiply.

The Bible says a new king arose which knew not Joseph, and he was jealous of the abundance and prosperity of the children of Israel and ordered taskmasters to afflict them. This constitutes the fulfillment of the prophecy given to Abram by God concerning his descendants being afflicted in a strange land. In the fullness of time, the Lord raised up a deliverer named Moses. He was an Israelite who grew up in the house of Pharaoh. Moses was raised up by God to deliver his people out of bondage and establish a sacrificial system that would enable the people to receive pardon for their transgressions.

Now that we have looked at a very brief history of the period between Abram and Moses, let us examine the establishment of the sacrifices instituted by God. Keep in mind that these sacrifices would be a type and a shadow of the ultimate sacrifice that would be made by the promised seed.

When God was ready to deliver His people from the bondage of Egypt, He gave His servant Moses explicit instructions on how the people should prepare. (Ex 12:1-7).

God told Moses that the only way the death angel would pass a house is if blood was on the two side posts and on the upper doorpost of the house, over the door. The blood had to be from a lamb without spot or blemish. Egypt was a place of bondage, and deliverance was instituted by the shedding of the blood of a lamb without blemish.

After God delivered the people with a mighty hand, He instructed Moses to ordain his brother Aaron as the high priest. Aaron would minister before Him in order to obtain atonement for the sins of the people via sacrificial offerings. *"And if his offering be of the flocks, namely, of the sheep, or of the goats, for a burnt sacrifice; he shall bring it a male without blemish"* (Leviticus 1:10). The Lord instituted five offerings for the altar of sacrifice, because five is the number in scripture that represents grace. We are saved by grace through faith.

1) *The burnt offering.* The premier offering given on the altar of sacrifice. The priests would keep the skin and everything else had to be burned, with only the ashes remaining. The priests receiving the skin paint a wonderful picture of the covering God made for Adam and Eve out of animal's skin.
2) *The Peace offering.* The promised seed would restore peace between God and man.
3) *The Sin Offering.* The promised seed is seen here as the substitute for us.
4) *The trespass offering.* This offering was two-fold in that it covered trespasses against God and our neighbors.
5) *The meat offering.* Typifies the humanity of the promised seed.

It is only through the shedding of blood that we have remission of sins. *"And almost all things are by the law purged with blood; and without shedding of blood is no remission"* (Hebrews 9:22).

This is the key component, which separates Christianity from all other faiths. There can be no remission of sin without the shedding of blood. As I mentioned earlier, God's institution of the blood sacrifice as recorded in the book of Leviticus was a shadow and a type of a larger plan of salvation. In order to access salvation, the sinner needs to repent of their sins so the blood of Jesus can cleanse them. In order to manifest this plan, God would have to bring forth the promised seed of the woman, because the high priest who entered into the holy of holies with blood would have to offer a sacrifice for his own sins first. The seed of the woman would be sinless so he would be able to offer himself a sacrifice once and for all. He would have no need to offer any sacrifices for himself because he would be the Lamb without a blemish.

In the fullness of time, the Lord sent His angel Gabriel to a virgin espoused to a man named Joseph. *"And in the sixth month the angel Gabriel was sent from God unto a city of Galilee, named Nazareth, To a virgin espoused to a man whose name was Joseph, of the house of David; and the virgin's name was Mary. And the angel came in unto her, and said, Hail, thou that art highly favored, the Lord is with thee: blessed art thou among women. And when she saw him, she was troubled at his saying, and cast in her mind what manner of salutation this should be. And the angel said unto her, 'Fear not, Mary: for thou hast found favor with God. And, behold, thou shalt conceive in thy womb, and bring forth a son, and shalt call his name JESUS. He shall be great, and shall be called the Son of the Highest: and the Lord God shall give unto him the throne of his father David: And he shall reign over the house of Jacob for ever; and of his kingdom there shall be no end.' Then said Mary unto the angel, 'how shall this be, seeing I know not a man?' And the angel answered and said unto her, 'The Holy Ghost shall come upon thee, and the power of the Highest shall overshadow thee: therefore also that holy thing which shall be born of thee shall be called the Son of Go."* (Luke 1: 26-35).

What a wonderful fulfillment of the promise of a seed. He would be great, He would be the son of the most high, and His kingdom would have no end. The reason why He had to be the seed of a woman was because God would be his Father. Like the lamb without blemish, He could not have the sinful nature of an earthly father, because He could not be the propitiation for our sins if He had a sin nature. Although He was born to be King, his first crib was a manger in a stable of animals. In the natural, it does not seem like a proper entrance into the world for one who would be the Son of the Most High, but God has chosen the foolish things of this world to confound the wise. His humble birthplace is a testament to the fact that He can identify with human beings trapped in situations that make them live like animals.

When it was time for His public ministry, He came to the Jordan where his cousin John the Baptist was baptizing people. The religious leaders sent priests and Levites to ask John who he was. John's response when he saw Jesus is an awesome confirmation and fulfillment of the salvation God promised to mankind. *"And they asked him, and said unto him, Why baptizest thou then, if thou be not that Christ, nor Elias, neither that prophet? John answered them, saying, I baptize with water: but there standeth one among you, whom ye know not; He it is, who coming after me is preferred before me, whose shoe's latchet I am not worthy to unloose. These things were done in Bethabara beyond Jordan, where John was baptizing. The next day John seeth Jesus coming unto him, and saith, Behold the Lamb of God, which taketh away the sin of the world. This is he of whom I said, After me cometh a man which is preferred before me: for he was before me. And I knew him not: but that he should be made manifest to Israel, therefore am I come baptizing with water. And John bare record, saying, I saw the Spirit descending from heaven like a dove, and it abode upon him. And I knew him not: but he that sent me to baptize with water, the same said unto me, Upon whom thou shalt see the Spirit descending, and remaining on him, the same is he which baptizeth with the Holy Ghost. And I saw, and bare record that this is the Son of God" (John 1:25-34).*

God fulfilled His promise to provide a seed by sending His only begotten son to die on the cross. His heel was bruised when He was crucified, but He bruised the serpent's head when He arose triumphantly on the third day, and took the keys of death, hell, and the grave from Satan. Because of His death, burial, and resurrection, men and women no longer have to suffer the torments of the Devil and his minions. They can believe in the Lord Jesus and receive freedom from the power and the penalty of sin, Hallelujah! Jesus shed His blood not only to provide salvation, but also to start us on a journey of sanctification and glorification. Salvation is the beginning of the journey, not the end of it. Many people receive salvation and don't press on to know the Lord intimately. He has so much more for us than simply escaping the wrath to come. He wants to bring us to a place of perfection. The perfecting process will come to fruition through the church He is building.

CHAPTER 5
THE CHURCH

"When Jesus came into the coasts of Caesarea Philippi, he asked his disciples, saying, whom do men say that I the Son of man am? And they said, some say that thou art John the Baptist: some, Elias; and others, Jeremias, or one of the prophets. He saith unto them, But whom say ye that I am? And Simon Peter answered and said, Thou art the Christ, the Son of the living God. And Jesus answered and said unto him, Blessed art thou, Simon Barjona: for flesh and blood hath not revealed it unto thee, but my Father which is in heaven. And I say also unto thee, that thou art Peter, and upon this rock I will build my church; and the gates of hell shall not prevail against it" (Matthew 16:13–18).

Jesus asked his disciples a very important question when he came into the coasts of Caesarea Philippi. He asked them, *"Whom do men say that I the Son of man am?"* Jesus did not ask the question because He was ignorant of what those outside His inner circle and those inside His inner circle thought about Him. The question was asked to bring forth a powerful revelation to His disciples of His identity, and His purpose. The answer to the question was in the question itself. He said, *"I the Son of Man."* The term Son of Man had Messianic implications. Daniel wrote, *"I saw in the night visions, and, behold, one like the Son of man came with the clouds of heaven, and came to the Ancient of days, and they brought him near before him. And there was given him dominion, and glory, and a kingdom, that all people, nations, and languages, should serve him: his dominion is an everlasting dominion, which shall not pass away, and his kingdom that which shall not be destroyed." (Daniel 7:13-14).* The vision Daniel saw concerning the Son of Man confirms what the Angel Gabriel said to Mary when he came to tell her she would carry the promised seed. He said to her, *"and the Lord God shall give unto him the throne of his father David: And he shall reign over the house of Jacob for ever; and of his kingdom there shall be no end"* (Luke 1:32b, 33).

The disciples were ignorant of Jesus' true identity, although they spent several years being trained by Him. It is no different today; many people profess to know Him but in actuality, they do not have a true revelation of who He is. The answers the disciples gave Jesus, is proof the people at that time only had a partial idea of His identity. Some thought He was John the Baptist: some, Elias; and others, Jeremias, or one of the prophets. At least they were in the ballpark when they suggested He was one of the prophets. The Muslims believe He is just a Prophet; other religions believe He was a good person, but He is so much more than any title we have to describe Him.

After hearing what men thought about His identity, Jesus narrows the focus and puts the question to the disciples by saying, *"Who do you say that I am?"* (Matthew 16:15b). Simon Peter answered and said, *"Thou art the Christ, the Son of the Living God"* (Matthew 16:16). Peter's answer was an apostolic revelation from the throne of God, for it elicited this response from Jesus: *"And Jesus answered and said unto him, 'Blessed art thou, Simon Barjona: for flesh and blood hath not revealed it unto thee, but my Father which is in heaven. And I say also unto thee, That thou art Peter, and upon this rock I will build my church; and the gates of hell shall not prevail against it. And I will give unto thee the keys of the kingdom of heaven: and whatsoever thou shalt bind on earth shall be bound in heaven: and whatsoever thou shalt loose on earth shall be loosed in heaven'"* (Matthew 16:17–19).

We will never receive Godly revelation concerning Jesus from the flesh. Flesh and blood can give us partial truths or hearsay from men, but if we want true revelation, we must receive it from the Holy Spirit. We must remember that the church is being built by Jesus, not man. Many people associate the word church with a building or a denomination. I often hear people say they have a storefront church, or they go to a Baptist, Pentecostal, or Methodist Church. I pause here for another emphatic statement. The word *My* is the only word Jesus placed before the word church. The structure of the building does not matter—it could be a cathedral, or it could be a storefront, or someone's living room. The building is the meeting place of the church and not the church itself. The body of Christ has divided into camps and given themselves denominational names like Pentecostals,

Anglicans, and Episcopalians, based on their interpretation of the word of God.

In order to eradicate the erroneous teachings concerning the church, we must define the word church and the purpose Jesus has for it. The word church in the Greek is *Ek-klay-see-ah*, meaning "a calling out." It is a compound word from the primary preposition *ek*. According to Strong's Concordance, *ek* denotes origin, the point whence motion or action proceeds, from, out of place, time, or cause. The word *Kal-eh-o* means, "To call." The purpose of God's call and the building of the church are summed up in this statement, *"Ye also, as lively stones, are built up a spiritual house, an holy priesthood, to offer up spiritual sacrifices, acceptable to God by Jesus Christ" (1 Peter 2:5).* In verse 9, Peter goes on to say, *"But ye are a chosen generation, a royal priesthood, an holy nation, a peculiar people; that you should show forth the praises of him who has called you out of darkness into his marvelous light"* God is calling a people out of darkness to sanctify and consecrate them as priests. Sanctification is not determined by a certain dress code or look. It is the process by which we are conformed to the image and likeness of Jesus. Consecration is the setting apart of someone or something for use by God. This sanctified and consecrated people will radiate the praises and glory of God throughout eternity. Each and every person called by Jesus and washed in His blood is added to the building as a lively stone.

Jesus was careful to mention that the gates of hell would try to prevail against the church, but He assures every believer that it will not prevail. In ancient times, the gate was a meeting place where important decisions were made. It was a gathering place where men of renown, and stature met to discuss matters of importance, and to transact business.

Jesus is letting us know that hell will not prevail against the individuals He has called. It does not matter the rank, or position of authority of the spirits that are dispatched against the called out ones. It is imperative that believers understand and apply that statement by Jesus. There are times when it might appear that the minions of hell have the upper hand because of what we are going through. This is the reason why God told Paul that His grace was sufficient when the Apostle was under attack by a high-ranking demon.

Jesus' statement concerning the gates of hell should be an

indication to the believer that there will be times of warfare as this glorious building is being erected—we must not be ignorant of that fact. Jesus used the word gates because there are different ranks in the demonic realm. The demonic spirit assigned to attack a young Christian is not as powerful as the one assigned to attack a seasoned one. We must not succumb to some of the unbalanced teachings on prosperity that have crept into the church. A construction sight is not a pretty sight. It is a place that is cordoned off, and there is frustration because of the logjam of traffic. There is a lot of dust and debris, not to mention the excessive noise associated with it. This is a picture of our life as Jesus Christ works in us to get out the gunk and the junk stored up in our trunk. We will have setbacks during the construction phase, but please, when you experience a setback, do not take a step back, because God is working on your comeback. When someone criticizes you for some slip up, tell him or her, "Be patient with me because I am under construction." Jesus Christ is the one constructing us, beloved; He is the Architect, and the blueprint is a replica of Him.

He is the foundation and cornerstone of the building. A building is only as strong as its foundation. We are strong in the Lord because He is the Rock and Foundation upon which our faith is built. Random House Webster's Collegiate Dictionary defines foundation as, *1) The basis or ground work of any thing. 2) The natural or prepared base or base on which some structure rests. 3) The lowest division of a building, wall, or the like.* In chapter two, I discussed the fact that faith is the substance of things hoped for and the evidence of things not seen. The substance and the evidence is that Jesus Christ is the foundation stone upon which our faith rests. Because He is that Rock, our faith can stand any test that attempts to shake it. Jesus told Peter, *"upon this rock I will build my church and the gates of hell shall not prevail against it."* (Luke 16b 18b) Roman Catholicism uses this particular verse to defend papal authority by saying Peter was the first pope. Was Jesus anointing Peter as the first of many popes based on that revelation?

Jesus told Peter that flesh and blood had not revealed it to him, but His Father in Heaven. The "It" Jesus refers to is the church being built on the revelation that Jesus is the Messiah sent from God; He is a foundation that cannot be shaken or destroyed. There is no way that God would use any sinful person such as Peter to be the foundation of the Church. The foundation of the church had to be strong enough to sustain the promise given to Abraham by God. According to the promise, the families of the earth would be blessed by Abraham's obedience. His descendants would be innumerable like the sand on the seashore. The best evidence for Christ being the foundation, the Rock upon which believers are being built, is the Word of God. Let us take a moment to examine some scriptures that deal with the word foundation. *Isaiah 28:16*, says, *"Therefore thus saith the Lord God, Behold, I lay in Zion for a foundation a stone, a tried stone, a precious corner stone, a sure foundation: he that believeth shall not make haste."* What a beautiful picture of the Messiah as the sure foundation. According to The Dictionary of Bible and Religion, Zion is the rock outcropping at the southern tip of the ridge between the Kidron and Tyropoeon valleys in Jerusalem. The Rock was the site of Abraham's attempted sacrifice of Isaac. On this rock, David set up an altar of sacrifice, and Solomon built Yahweh's Temple. The second Temple, reared by Ezra and Nehemiah, and beautified by Herod the Great in Jesus' time, also stood on Mount Zion. Zion is called the city of God.

Beloved, Zion is not only a place; it is also a people. Jesus is the foundation stone being laid in a people. In John 2:19, the religious leaders asked for a sign when Jesus cleared the temple of the merchandisers. He said to them, *"Destroy this temple, and in three days I will raise it up."* Their response was, *"Forty and six years was this temple in building, and wilt thou rear it up in three days?"* They did not understand that Jesus was referring to His body. His body would be beaten, battered, and bruised, but be resurrected in three days. God tested and tried that Rock, that Stone, before He laid it as our foundation.

"For other foundation can no man lay than that is laid, which is Jesus Christ" *(1 Corinthians 3:11).* No man could have laid the foundation, and no man can be the foundation upon which the Church of God is being built. Anyone who stands on any foundation less than the Lord Jesus Christ will crumble when the storms of adversity begin to rage.

We can stand because God dug a deep foundation for us. Picture in your mind the digging that takes place when a skyscraper is built. In order for that massive structure to withstand the elements, the builders have to dig very deep into

FIDEL M. DONALDSON

the earth. Not only does the skyscraper have to withstand the elements, but it also has to hold the weight of all the people and the equipment that it is built to hold. Our foundation was not laid overnight. In *Revelation 13:8b*, the Apostle John describes Jesus as the Lamb slain from the foundation of the world. It is impossible for the human mind to fathom the laying of the foundation of the world, because of the immensity of this world, yet the Lamb was slain from that time. Beloved, has Jesus not been tried and found worthy to keep us from falling?

Not only is Jesus the sure foundation, but according to Isaiah, He is the precious cornerstone. The cornerstone of any building is a very important stone. In Matthew 21:42, Jesus tells the parable of the wicked farmers in order to expose the murderous plot of the religious leaders. He said to them, *"Did you never read in the scriptures, The stone which the builders rejected, the same is become the head of the corner: this is the Lord's doing, and it is marvelous in our eyes?"*

Random House Webster's Collegiate Dictionary defines the word cornerstone as, "A stone representing the nominal starting place in the construction of a monumental building: The foundation on which something is constructed or developed." The Church of Jesus Christ is that monumental building because each believer is a lively stone that is layering the foundation. The Patriarch, and father of the faithful, Abraham, looked prophetically for this monumental building (Hebrews 11:9–10).

Jesus has established five offices to aid in the construction of this monumental building. Remember five is the number of grace, and it signifies the fact that He did not have to establish the five offices, because He is more than capable of smoothing out the stones by Himself. The offices He established are the office of the Apostle, the Prophet, the Evangelist, the Pastor, and the Teacher. The purpose for the establishment of these offices is found in *Ephesians, 4:7–13*: *"But unto every one of us is given grace according to the measure of the gift of Christ. Wherefore he saith, when he ascended up on high, he led captivity captive, and gave gifts unto men. (Now that he ascended, what is it but that he also descended first into the lower parts of the earth? He that descended is the same also that ascended up far above all heavens, that he might fill all things.) And he gave some, apostles; and some, prophets; and some, evangelists; and some, pastors and teachers; For the perfecting of the saints, for the work of the ministry, for the edifying of the body of Christ: Till we all come in the unity of the faith, and of the*

64

knowledge of the Son of God, unto a perfect man, unto the measure of the stature of the fullness of Christ."

Let us take this opportunity to examine the seven things Jesus will accomplish with what is called the five fold ministry, and remember seven is the number of perfection.

1...The perfecting of the saints: In describing the believer as living stones for God's house, Peter said we are built up a spiritual house, and holy priesthood, to offer up spiritual sacrifices, acceptable to God by Jesus. From the very beginning, God demanded that any sacrifice brought to Him had to be without spot or blemish. The cleansing power of the Blood of Jesus in the removal of our sins is for the purpose of preparing us to be the spiritual house God desires. People get uncomfortable when the word perfect is used, but is anything impossible for God. Is there any sin so filthy that the blood of Jesus cannot wash it away? Man is not capable of perfecting anything because he has inherent flaws, but God has no flaws so He is able to take that which is imperfect and perfect it. The weight and sin that doth so easily beset us will be eradicated before all is said and done. The word of God is true, and if God says the saints will be perfected, then so be it.

2...The work of the ministry: It is amazing how God will use the very saints He is perfecting to help in the perfecting process of others. Jesus established the five-fold ministry to do just that, to aid in the perfection of the saints, so the saints can do the work of the ministry. The words ministry and minister have been exalted to a status that was never intended by Jesus. We hear people talk all the time about their ministry. Ministers, whether they are Apostles, Prophets, Evangelist, Pastors, or Teachers, are often treated as if they are above the people. Some individuals actually get offended when you do not put their title before their name. By examining the root from which we get the words ministry and minister, I pray the reader will get a Biblical definition and understanding of these terms.

The word ministry, as it is used by the Apostle Paul in Ephesians 4:12, is the Greek word *dee-ak-on-ee-ah*, and it means "service, attendance (as a servant)." It comes from the Greek word *dee-ak-on-os*, and that word means, "a waiter (at table or in other menial duties)."

In Matthew 20:20–28, Jesus gives His disciples a profound

teaching on the true meaning of the word minister. *"Then came to him the mother of Zebedee's children with her sons, worshipping him, and desiring a certain thing of him. And he said unto her, What wilt thou? She saith unto him, Grant that these my two sons may sit, the one on thy right hand, and the other on the left, in thy kingdom. But Jesus answered and said, Ye know not what ye ask. Are ye able to drink of the cup that I shall drink of, and to be baptized with the baptism that I am baptized with? They say unto him, We are able. And he saith unto them, Ye shall drink indeed of my cup, and be baptized with the baptism that I am baptized with: but to sit on my right hand, and on my left, is not mine to give, but it shall be given to them for whom it is prepared of my Father. And when the ten heard it, they were moved with indignation against the two brethren. But Jesus called them unto him, and said, Ye know that the princes of the Gentiles exercise dominion over them, and they that are great exercise authority upon them. But it shall not be so among you: but whosoever will be great among you, let him be your minister; And whosoever will be chief among you, let him be your servant: Even as the Son of man came not to be ministered unto, but to minister, and to give his life a ransom for many."*

The mother of Zebedee's children wanted her sons to sit on the right and the left of Jesus in His Kingdom. Her son's were called the "sons of thunder" by Jesus. There was a time when they were traveling with Jesus and wanted to call fire down from heaven because they felt Jesus was being disrespected by some Samaritans. They were two serious hombres. Every mother should want the best for her children, and what better place is there to be than on the right and the left of Jesus? The problem was that her request shows their ignorance of Jesus' true ministry.

Palestine was under Roman occupation, and the Jews were looking for a leader who would break the Roman yoke and return them to the glory days experienced under King David and his son Solomon. They did not understand that the road to the establishment of the Kingdom would be through the cross. It is an indictment on the religious leaders of the day because the prophets had foretold that the Messiah would have to suffer. The people were not interested in a suffering Messiah. When she explained what she wanted, Jesus asked her a question. First, He told her that she did not know what she was asking for, and then He asked her if they could drink from the cup that He would drink, and be baptized with His baptism. To their credit, they said yes, and Jesus agreed with them by telling them they would do both. He explained to them that the place they requested was not His to give, but His father prepared it for a particular people.

The other disciples were angry with James and John when they found out what they requested of Jesus. I don't believe their anger stemmed from any sense of piety, or altruism. I believe it is a position they wanted for themselves, because these men tried to stop women and children from getting close to Jesus.

It is at that moment Jesus teaches them the true definition of a minister and the work of the ministry. Everyone that names the name of Jesus must embrace the teaching. The writer says, *"Jesus called them unto Him."* It appears that their indignation and infighting had caused them to be away from Jesus. You will never find Jesus in the midst of infighting and petty disputes. Jesus told them not to be like the princes of the gentiles who exercised dominion and authority over the people. He told them that whoever wanted to be great, had to be their minister, and the person who wanted to be chief, had to be a servant, because He did not come to be ministered to but to minister, and give His life a ransom for many.

When Jesus uses the word servant, it is the Greek word *doo-los*, and it means "slave." Jesus is telling these ambitious disciples that His ministry is to serve the people. If the King who created all things can humble himself and become a servant, who among us is justified in exalting his or her self above the very people He has called them to serve. It does not matter if we are called Apostles, Prophets, Evangelist, Pastors, or Teachers. We need to have the revelation of, "the bigger the title, the bigger the servant."

I've heard it said in some circles that the Apostle is over the other five fold ministers. *1Corinthians 12:28a.* says, *"And God has set some in the church, first apostles, secondarily prophets, thirdly teachers."* To gain a proper understanding, we have to look at the meaning of the word Apostle. The word in the Greek is *ap-os-tol-los*, and it means, "An ambassador of the gospel." It comes from the Greek word, *ap-os-tel-lo*, "to set apart, to send out." The apostle is not first in terms of importance, but first in the order of those sent. He is a pioneer or a trailblazer who is separated and sent in the power of the Holy Spirit. The purpose is to clear a territory of demonic infestation in order to facilitate the entrance of the gospel. The reference for this is found in Acts 13:1–3, which reads, *"Now there were in the church that was at Antioch certain prophets and teachers; as Barnabas, and Simeon that was called Niger, and Lucius of Cyrene, and Manaen, which had been brought up with Herod the tetrarch, and Saul. As they ministered to the Lord, and fasted, the Holy Ghost said, Separate me Barnabas and Saul for the work whereunto I have called them. And when they had fasted and prayed, and laid their hands on them, they sent them away."*

They traveled across the Mediterranean Sea, and while they were preaching the Word of God in an area called Paphos, they encountered a sorcerer. He was a false Prophet named Bar-jesus. He was with the deputy of the country. It is important to note that the sorcerer had attached himself to the leader of that territory, thus giving Satan control over the region. The deputy called for Barnabas and Saul because he wanted to hear the word of God, but Bar-jesus, who was also called Elymas the sorcerer, withstood them, seeking to turn away the deputy from the faith. The word of God tells us how the Apostle Paul handled the situation. *Verses 9–12: "Then Saul, (who also is called Paul,) filled with the Holy Ghost, set his eyes on him, and said, O full of all subtlety and all mischief, thou child of the devil, thou enemy of all righteousness, wilt thou not cease to pervert the right ways of the Lord? And now, behold, the hand of the Lord is upon thee, and thou shalt be blind, not seeing the sun for a season. And immediately there fell on him a mist and darkness; and he went about seeking some to lead him by the hand. Then the deputy, when he saw what was done, believed, being astonished at the doctrine of the Lord."*

In order for the Word of God to take root in Paphos, the Apostle, by the power of the Holy Spirit, had to blind the eye of the false prophet and sorcerer who was influencing the leader of that area. God will demonstrate miracles, signs, and wonders through the ministry of the apostle. He does not do this in order to exalt the apostolic office; He does it so others can see that Jesus is Lord, and demons are subject to His authority. The word "first" when used with the apostolic office must always denote "first" in service and commitment to Jesus. I do not believe there is an individual in the Bible that exemplified the attitude of a servant of Jesus more than the Apostle Paul. A cursory look at some of the things he wrote concerning the ministry of the apostle will confirm this. In writing to the Corinthian Church, in reference to how apostles and other ministers are approved as ministers of Jesus, he lists several things that God's ministers will experience. In *2nd Corinthian 6:3–5*, he wrote, *"Giving no offence in any thing, that the ministry be not blamed: But in all things approving ourselves as the ministers of God, in much patience, in afflictions, in necessities, in distresses, in stripes, in imprisonments, in tumults, in labors, in watchings, in fastings."*

The apostolic office is not about sitting on some oversized chair in expensive costumes and sweet smelling perfumes, barking out orders to underlings. It is about an individual's willingness to humble his or herself so the power of Jesus can be demonstrated in their ministry—not through lip service, intellect, or trickery, but through the true signs that follow an apostle ordained by Jesus.

In *1ˢᵗ Corinthians 2:1–5* he said to them, *"And I, brethren, when I came to you, came not with excellency of speech or of wisdom, declaring unto you the testimony of God. For I determined not to know any thing among you, save Jesus Christ, and him crucified. And I was with you in weakness, and in fear, and in much trembling. And my speech and my preaching was not with enticing words of man's wisdom, but in demonstration of the Spirit and of power: That your faith should not stand in the wisdom of men, but in the power of God."*

If Paul had gone to Paphos acting like some big shot, he would not have had the ability to withstand the sorcerer and get deliverance for the deputy of that country. Elymas the Sorcerer was the spiritual head of the man who ruled that territory, so he was able to influence that whole area spiritually. Demons are assigned different territories, such as neighborhoods, towns, cities, states, countries, and nations, depending on their rank. When Daniel prayed, his prayer was heard and the Angel Gabriel was dispatched, but he told Daniel that the Prince of Persia withstood him 21 days. The Archangel Michael had to come and clear the air so the answer could be delivered.

It is important to remember that the deputy did not believe because there was something special about the apostle. The Bible says, *"Then the deputy, when he saw what was done, believed, being astonished at the doctrine of the Lord" (Acts 13:12).* It was not the man that astonished him but the doctrine of the Lord. He saw the demonstration of the power of God through a true servant of God over the powers of darkness. It is never about the minister, but always about the Lord Jesus Christ and His doctrine. The Governor was used to seeing false signs and demonic wonders, but the power of the spoken word of God is what opened his eyes to the truth.

One of the earmarks of the early church, which facilitated its growth, was its adherence to the apostle's doctrine, which is the doctrine of Jesus. Acts 2:41–43 states, *"Then they that gladly received his word were baptized: and the same day there were added unto them about three thousand souls. And they continued steadfastly in the apostles' doctrine and fellowship, and in breaking of bread, and in prayers. And fear came upon every soul: and many wonders and signs were done by the apostles."*

3…The edifying of the Body of Christ: The word edify means, "to instruct or benefit, especially morally or spiritually; uplift; enlighten." The Body of Christ represents every believer who has received salvation by grace through faith in the finished work of Jesus. The five offices are given to the body to help in the building up of the body, not to mistreat it, or to impede its growth and development.

4…Unity of the faith: In His prayer for His disciples and for future believers as recorded in John 17:21, Jesus said, *"That they all may be one; as you, Father, are in me, and I in You, that they also may be one in us: that the world may believe that you have sent me."* The word unity means, "The state of being one; oneness. A whole or totality as combining all its parts. Absence of diversity; unvaried or uniform character: Oneness of mind." When it comes to our faith in Jesus Christ, we cannot allow schisms to tear us apart. Civilized people will disagree on some things, but in matters of the faith, we must endeavor to stand on the Word of God and unite as one.

I remember receiving an invitation to minister at a church in Brooklyn, New York. The associate pastor called me and started to ask me some questions. I had never met him before, but the nature of his questions made me aware that he wanted to know what I believed. Concerning Jesus, I said five things to him: I told him that I believed in His virgin birth, His sinless life, His vicarious and atoning death, His resurrection from the grave, and His return.

When I went to the church to minister, the Lord led me to a man sitting in the front. I went over to him to give him a word from the Lord. All I could get of my mouth was, "Sir, the Lord says." Before I could finish the sentence, the man shouted out, "The Lord ain't never did nothing for me." I realized immediately that any man that would make such a statement was under the influence of demons. I stepped back, closed my eyes, and took authority of the demons that were tormenting his mind. After I finished praying, I went to minister to some other people. When I finished ministering and handed the mike over to the associate pastor, he spoke to the congregation and said, "I know this is a man of God because that man came in here today with a gun saying he felt like killing somebody." When he said that, I said, "Lord, I would have been the first one the devil would have shot." He said to me, "That is why I told you to watch and pray."

Needless to say, I don't pray with my eyes closed anymore when I am ministering to people.

Jesus thought unity among believers was important enough for Him to pray for it. The Apostle Paul was acutely aware of the dangers of individuals that would try to create schisms in the body, so he warned the believers. In his farewell to the elders of Ephesus, as recorded in *Acts 20:28–30*, he said, *"Take heed therefore unto yourselves, and to all the flock, over the which the Holy Ghost has made you overseers, to feed the church of God, which he has purchased with his own blood. For I know this, that after my departing shall grievous wolves enter in among you, not sparing the flock. Also of your own selves shall men arise, speaking perverse things, to draw away disciples after them."* Attempts to break the cohesion of the body will arise internally and externally. It is up to the elders to watch and pray so the attempt will come to naught.

5…Knowledge of the Son of God: In order to come into a deep knowledge of the Son of God, we must be willing to go through the things the apostle described to the *Philippians 3:8-10.* We must be willing to lose all things to gain that knowledge. There should be nothing in our lives so important to us that we are unwilling to part with it if the Lord instructs us to do so.

Jesus spoke to a rich young man, as recorded in Matthew 19:16–23, Mark 10:17–31, and Luke 18:18–30. The young man came to Jesus asking him what good thing he should do to inherit eternal life. He was under the misguided notion that eternal life is gained through good works. He actually called Jesus, Good Master. Jesus told him, *"If he would enter into life he should keep the commandments."* He asked Jesus which ones he should keep, and Jesus told him not to murder, commit adultery, steal, or bear false witness. He also told him to honor his mother and father, and to love his neighbor as himself. The young man told Jesus that he had done all those things from his youth, but he was lacking something and he wanted Jesus to tell him what it was. I believe Jesus knew the young man attempted to keep the commandments in order to receive justification, and He told him that to teach him a valuable lesson. Jesus told him if he would be perfect, he should go and sell all that he had, and give the proceeds to the poor. In doing so, he would have treasure in heaven and would be able to follow Jesus.

Verse 22 of Matthew 19 says, *"But when the young man heard that saying, he went away sorrowful: for he had great possessions."* Jesus told his disciples that a rich man shall hardly enter into the kingdom of heaven. It was not the fact that the man was rich that stopped him from following Jesus, and entering into kingdom living, it was his unwillingness to obey what Jesus instructed him to do. Anything in our lives that obscures our vision of the knowledge of Jesus becomes an idol and a god to us.

6...A Perfect Man: The previous illustration is a fitting preface to the word perfect. Some people are perplexed by the word perfect because they do not understand the different ways the word is used in the scriptures. How many times have you heard someone say, "He or she thinks they are perfect?" How many times have you heard someone say, "I am not perfect," using that phrase in order to excuse some mistake or lapse of judgment? The guilt and the stain of sin lead many people to believe Godly perfection is impossible to achieve. My question to the reader is, "Is there anything too hard for God?" Is the sin nature inherited from our ancestor, Adam, more powerful than the cleansing power of the Blood of Jesus?

The word perfect, as it is used by the Apostle Paul in *Ephesians 4:13*, is the Greek word *tel-i-os*, and it means "complete (in various applications of labor, growth, mental and moral character, etc)." The word *tel-i-os* comes from the Greek word *tel-os*, and it means, "to set out for a definite point or goal." How wonderful it is to know that God has raised us up from the pit of sin by extending mercy and grace towards us. He has done it in order to help us reach the goal. The goal is perfection in Jesus Christ, and nothing less. Perfection in Christ should be the ultimate goal of everyone that loves him. Do not allow your human frailties and weaknesses to cause you to doubt the word of God. I beseech you to remember the words written by the Apostle John in *1 John 3:2*: *"Beloved, now are we the sons of God, and it doth not yet appear what we shall be: but we know that, when he shall appear, we shall be like him; for we shall see him as he is."*

In the section on the Blood of Jesus: the Lamb of God, I discussed the fact that sin means, "Missing the mark." Another way of saying it is, sin is "missing the goal." The Blood of Jesus cleanses us of our sin, and He established the five-fold ministry to bring us from a place of infancy to maturity, or perfection. The goal is the prize of the high calling described by Paul in Philippians 3:13–15. Let's examine some other examples of how the word perfect is used in the Bible. *Genesis 6:9b* says, *"Noah was a just man and perfect in his generations, and Noah walked with God."* The Hebrew word for perfect as it is used here is *taw-meem*, and it means, "Integrity, truth, and whole." Someone might ask the question, "Isn't Noah the one who was drunk and naked in the ark?" The answer is yes, but that does not negate the fact that the Bible said he was perfect in his generations; on the contrary, it shows how wicked and debauched his generation was. Noah was whole and complete because he walked with God, and when an individual is walking with God, he is walking in fullness and integrity. Does this mean the person will not stumble occasionally? Absolutely not! When he stumbles, he understands that God is able to pick him up, clean him up, and aid him in the continuance of his journey.

Job 1:1 says, *"There was a man in the land of Uz, whose name was Job; and that man was perfect and upright, and one that feared God, and eschewed evil."* Perfect as it is used here is the word *tawm*, and it means, "complete; usually morally." Job's morality did not exclude him from being attacked by Satan. Every member of the body of Christ will experience attacks from the enemy, but be of good courage, and know that *Romans 8:28* says, *"And we know that all things work together for good to them that love God, to them who are the called according to his purpose."* Because God has called us, and has a great purpose for us, He will work everything in our lives for our good. Every good and bad experience will be used for the purpose of God for our lives; keep in mind what that purpose is. The seventh item in the list given by the Apostle Paul in Ephesians 4:11–13 will help us to understand the purpose of God for our lives.

73

7…Measure of the Stature of the Fullness of Christ: The purpose of the five offices given to the Church by Jesus is encapsulated here. Random House Webster's College Dictionary defines the word measure as, "the extent, dimensions, or quantity, etc., of something, ascertained especially by comparison with a standard." The word stature is defined as, "the height of a human or esteem or status based on one's positive qualities or achievements." Beloved, the person we are being perfected to measure up to and the standard for that measurement is none other than the Lord Jesus. Once He chooses us as one of the lively stones to fit us jointly in the building, He will continue to smooth our rough edges until there are no defects, inside or out. We will not measure up to His standard, or come into His fullness for our lives unless we are willing to turn over the rough places in our lives to Him.

All of us have things in us that we need Him to deal with. For some it might be pride, anger, jealousy, envy, backbiting, lust, etc. In *John 14:30b,* Jesus said, *"For the prince of this world cometh, and has nothing in me."* There was no opening in Jesus for the adversary to take hold, because Jesus was full of the Holy Spirit, and had the measure and the stature of God. Believe it or not, He is perfecting sons and daughters who will walk in the same measure and stature. This perfecting process is not about being born again, and waiting to die and go to heaven. There is a lot more to the building of the church than that. The sons and daughters of God will be manifested in this earth, and they will help Jesus to destroy the works of darkness. He does not need their help, but His use of them is a vindication for man.

Sin entered into the world through man, and God sent His Son, a man, to pay the debt for men. His Son is now using men and women in these last days to deliver the earth from the bondage and the plague of sin. It is time for the church to embrace the revelation of the manifestation of the sons of God. The manifestation will be in demonstration and power of the Holy Spirit. The power is not given to the sons of God for them to be heavenly minded and no earthly good. When Adam sinned, Satan was allowed to operate in the world as the father of the children of rebellion. The world is full of rebellion right now, and anyone who does not see that is deceived. There will be a Kairos moment when Jesus will release His manifested sons in this earth.

Please allow the scriptures to confirm this. *Romans 8:18–22* states, *"For I reckon that the sufferings of this present time are not worthy to be compared with the glory which shall be revealed in us. For the earnest expectation of the creature waiteth for the manifestation of the sons of God. For the creature was made subject to vanity, not willingly, but by reason of him who hath subjected the same in hope, Because the creature itself also shall be delivered from the bondage of corruption into the glorious liberty of the children of God. For we know that the whole creation groaneth and travaileth in pain together until now."*

The Apostle does not say that Heaven is groaning and travailing; on the contrary, the earth is groaning and in travail, because of sin. Religion does not have the answer or the solution for this crisis. The only solution is Jesus Christ, and the power He is giving His sons who are willing to endure suffering for His name.

The raising of Lazarus from the dead gives us a wonderful picture of the breaking of the bondage of sin and death. The story of Lazarus is recorded in John 11. When Jesus received the news that his friend Lazarus was sick, His response was, *"This sickness is not unto death, but for the glory of God, that the Son of God might be glorified thereby."* Jesus is the only one who can get glory out of a dead situation. Jesus stayed two more days at the place where He was, when He received the news of Lazarus' sickness. Two is the number of witness, and the people in the town where Lazarus lived were about to witness the glory of God manifested through His Son. When Jesus arrived, He found that Lazarus was in the grave for four days. In Biblical Mathematics page 60, Evangelist Ed Vallowe writes, "Four is the number of creation and God's creative work. The material creation was finished on the fourth day. In the first and second chapters of Genesis, in the record of creation, the word creature is found four times. *Romans 8:19–22*, the words creature and creation are used four times in succession. Revelation 4:6–8, John saw four living creatures around the throne of God. *Revelation 5:13*, the creatures in four different places ascribe four words of praise to the Father and to Jesus Christ."

Jesus knew before He arrived that Lazarus was dead, and He told it to His disciples. One of Lazarus' sisters came to meet Jesus and told Him that her brother would not have died if Jesus had been there. She then expresses tremendous faith in Jesus when she says, *"But I know, that even now, whatsoever you will ask of God, God will give it to you."* Jesus said unto her, *"Your brother shall rise again."* *(John 11:23)* She was under the impression that Jesus meant her brother would rise again in the resurrection at the last day. At this point, Jesus states emphatically, *"I am the resurrection, and the life: he that believes in me, though he were dead, yet shall he live: And whosoever lives and believes in me shall never die, do you believe this?"* Here is a verse that represents the manifestation of the resurrection of the sons of God. Lazarus is a type of the sons of God who will be resurrected as a first fruit offering to God. These sons are the individuals who have proven themselves faithful as servants and are now called sons. They are called sons because they have the mind of Christ, and know His Father's business.

Martha understood that Jesus had the ability to raise her brother from the dead because she had a revelation of who Jesus was. *Verse 27* states, *"She said unto him, yes, Lord: I believe that you are the Christ, the Son of God, which should come into the world."* Martha told her sister Mary that Jesus was in the area, and Mary went out to see him. Many of the Jews followed her, and when she found Jesus, she fell at his feet weeping. She told Jesus the same thing her sister Martha told him: *"Lord, if you had been here, my brother would not have died."*

Jesus, not being one to waste words, does not go into detail about the resurrection with her as He did with Martha. When He saw all the weeping that was taking place, the Bible says, *"He groaned in the spirit, and was troubled."* I believe this is an instance, referred to in scripture as deep calling unto deep. *Psalm 42:7* states, *"Deep calleth unto deep at the noise of thy waterspouts: all thy waves and thy billows are gone over me."* The Spirit of God was being stirred in Jesus in preparation for the resurrection of Lazarus.

Water is a type of the Holy Spirit, and Jesus had the Spirit without measure. At that Kairos moment, Jesus became the waterspout out of which the Holy Spirit would raise Lazarus from the grave. I am firmly convinced that the groaning of Jesus was His use of His heavenly language, a language we call tongues or *glossolalia*. This language is heard when we are filled with the Spirit and He gives us utterance. Jesus was about to pray in the power of the Holy Spirit.

In Romans 8, the Apostle Paul made it clear that we are groaning and travailing in pain like the rest of creation. He says in verse 23, *"And not only they, but ourselves also, which have the first fruits of the Spirit, even we ourselves groan within ourselves, waiting for the adoption, to wit, the redemption of our body."* In verse 26 he states, *"likewise the Spirit also helps our infirmities: for we know not what we should pray for as we ought, but the Spirit maketh intercession for us with groanings which cannot be uttered."* The resurrection prayer of Jesus could not be prayed in the common vernacular; it had to be prayed in the power of the Spirit.

There was tumult and mayhem at the gravesite of Lazarus. Everyone was weeping, moaning, and wailing. Jesus himself wept, probably over their unbelief. Some of the Jews commented on the fact that He loved Lazarus, while others said, *"could not this man, which opened the eyes of the blind, have caused that even this man should not have died?"* The Bible says Jesus groaned again in himself and came to the grave. The grave was a cave that was covered by a stone.

Jesus told the people to take away the stone, and Martha replied that her brother had been in the grave four days, and was stinking. Beloved, it does not matter the length of time or the deadness of your situation. Jesus is able to give you a resurrection miracle. His response to Martha was, *"Said I not unto you, that, if you would believe, you should see the glory of God?"* The sons of God will manifest His Glory in the earth. When the stone was removed, Jesus lifted up his eyes and said, *"Father, I thank you that you heard me. And I know that you always hear me: but because of the people which stand by I said it, that they may believe that you have sent me."*

When Jesus was groaning in the spirit, He was speaking a heavenly language to His Father, and His Father heard him. Now He was about to speak so the people would hear and believe. The Bible says, *"He cried out with a loud voice, "Lazarus, come forth."* He spoke three words because three is the number of resurrection. In *John 2:19,* Jesus said, *"Destroy this temple, and in three days I will raise it up."* There are three recorded cases found in the Old Testament of people being raised from the dead. The first was that of the son of the widow of Zarephath. The second was the raising of the Shunamite woman's son by the Prophet Elisha, and the third was the dead body that came to life when it was thrown into the sepulcher of Elisha.

When Jesus called him forth, the Bible says, *"And he that was dead came forth, bound hand and foot with grave clothes: and his face was*

bound about with a napkin. Jesus said unto them, loose him and let him go."
Although Lazarus was resurrected, he was still bound by the
grave clothes. When a sinner calls on the name of Jesus for
salvation, his spirit man comes alive but his mind is not
completely renewed in an instant. There is a process called
sanctification. It is imperative to note, Jesus does not loose him
from his grave clothes. He told the people to do it. In his
teachings on the sons of God, Dr. Greene says they will walk in
the power of the Holy Spirit, and will loose creation, and the
creature from their grave clothes of sin.

CHAPTER 6
THE POWER OF THE HOLY SPIRIT

"*On the last day, that great day of the feast, Jesus stood and cried, saying, If any man thirst, let him come unto me, and drink. He that believeth on me, as the scripture hath said, out of his belly shall flow rivers of living water. But this spake he of the Spirit, which they that believe on him should receive: for the Holy Ghost was not yet given; because that Jesus was not yet glorified" (John 7:37–39).*

The Holy Spirit, the third person of the Godhead, is given to the church as a teacher, a guide, and a comforter. He is the one who is active in the empowerment of the believers, and is working in them to complete their sanctification. He empowers the believer to withstand the attacks of the Devil. A believer will not be able to complete the mandate of God for his or her life without being baptized with the Holy Spirit. It takes the power of the Holy Spirit to overcome the fleshly lust, against which we wrestle. Jesus likens the Spirit to rivers of living waters. It is such an important event that Jesus waited until the last day, that great day of the feast, to stand and cry out. When Jesus cries out, the matter is of utmost importance.

In Rivers of Living Waters Page 60 Gene Cunningham writes, Jesus was attending the Feast of Tabernacles, as recorded in *John 7: 2, 10, and 15.* The itinerary for this great feast consisted of the priests carrying water from the pool of Siloam to the Temple. The water would be poured over the altar as a symbol of the cleansing power of the Lamb of God, who would take away the sins of the world *(John 1:29, 36).* On the eighth day, there was a solemn assembly. At this assembly, the multitude would stand in silent contemplation. The ritual of water was not carried out, indicating that the cleansing could not be provided until the

Messiah of God came. Jesus used the time of silence to cry out an invitation for the thirsty to come to him and drink.

The Holy Spirit gives us a beautiful picture of this thirst-quenching water in the story of the woman at the well *(John 4: 13-14)*. She had lived her life trying to satisfy her thirst by going from one man to another. When she encountered Jesus at the well, He offered her living water, but she thought He meant natural water. When she asked Jesus to give her some of that water, He told her to go and return with her husband. She confessed to Jesus that she had no husband, and Jesus said to her, *"Thou hast well said, I have no husband: for thou has had five husbands; and he whom thou now has is not thy husband: in that sadist thou truly."*

Five husbands signify her need for grace, but she could not receive grace from a natural man. This fact is proven because she had a sixth man when she met Jesus, and still was empty. Jesus represents the seventh man, and seven is the number of perfection. Jesus was the only man who could perfect her and give her eternal life and rivers of living water.

When she came to the well, she had her water pot. Her water pot represented the human attempt at cleansing and thirst quenching. Jesus had explained to her that, *"Whoever drank the natural water would thirst again, but whoever drinks of the water that he gives would never thirst. The water He gives shall be in them a well of water springing up into everlasting life."* When she received the true revelation of Jesus, and the rivers of living water, her life was totally transformed. She came to the well with a sullied reputation because of all the men in her life. The Bible says she left her water pot and went into the city and said to the men, *"come, see a man, which told me all things that ever I did: Is not this the Christ?"*

The word Christ in the Greek is *Kristos*, and it means, "Anointed." It comes from the Greek word *khree-o*, which means, "to smear or rub with oil, to consecrate to an office." Her contact with Jesus facilitated the breaking of the yokes that had her bound. The Prophet Isaiah said, *"The yoke shall be destroyed because of the anointing"* *(Isaiah 10:27)*. *Acts 10:38* states, *"How God anointed Jesus of Nazareth with the Holy Ghost and with power, who went about doing good and healing all that were oppressed of the devil; for God was with Him."* Jesus had the Spirit without measure, and that allowed Him to break the yoke of oppression from all who encountered Him.

The response of the men of her village to her question, *"is this not the Christ,"* *(John 4:29b)* Provides proof of the radical change in her life. The Bible says, *"Then they went out of the city, and came unto Him" (John 4:30).* The woman that returned to the village was not the same woman who left, because the men could see her transformation. They realized that the man to whom she was referring was not the same as all the other men with whom she had cavorted. They came out to meet Jesus because of the woman's message. Her message was simple, yet profound. It was a message made up of three simple, yet life changing statements: *1) "Come see a Man." 2) "Which told me all things that ever I did?" 3) "Is not this the Christ?"* When she used the word, "the Christ," the men of the village knew she meant the one anointed who could destroy the yokes, and set them free from the oppression of the devil.

This is repudiation and an indictment on anyone who believes women should not be preachers. She was doing the work of an evangelist when she returned to the village. Her anointed message was the catalyst that led Jesus to go to her village and tarry there for two days. Two is the number of witness, and when Jesus arrived at her village, He gave witness to her message. Her transformed life was a testimony of the fact that lives change when Jesus reveals himself to people, and they receive rivers of living water.

It is safe to infer that the lives of the men, women, and children were changed when Jesus stayed there. Wherever Jesus went people were healed, and demons were cast out. The world does not need great religious orators, or men with enticing words. The world needs a simple, profound, Spirit-filled message about the life changing power of Jesus.

The adversary will do anything to keep us subject to the carnal man so we are unable to drink from the rivers Jesus has provided through the Holy Spirit. Many believers are drying up, and dying of thirst in the midst of a reservoir. They are bound by the spirit of religion, a spirit of deception, and a spirit of apathy. God is manifesting Himself in a company of people who are full of joy, because they are drinking from the river. Ps 46:4–5 states, *"There is a river, the streams whereof shall make glad the city of God, the holy place of the tabernacles of the most High. God is in the midst of her; she shall not be moved: God shall help her and that right early."* The city of God is not only a place but it is also a people. It is a holy people being prepared as a bride for Christ. They are full of the joy of the Lord because they are drinking from the river, and have become tabernacles for God.

In Genesis 26:14–25, we find a beautiful picture of how the believer overcomes the enemies' attempts to plug the wells Jesus has provided for us. The story deals with Isaac the son of Abraham and his battles with the Philistines, who tried to plug all the wells that Abraham's servants dug. Genesis 26:14–16 states, *"For he had of flocks, and possessions of herds, and great store of servants: and the Philistines envied him. For all the wells, which his father's servants had dug in the days of Abraham his father, the Philistines had stopped them, and filled them with earth. And Abimelech said unto Isaac; Go from us; for thou art much mightier than we. And Isaac departed thence, and pitched his tent in the valley of Gerar, and dwelt there."*

A) *Gerar* means, "A rolling country." A rolling country speaks of the hills and valleys every believer will experience on the path to perfection.

Verses 18–20 states, *"And Isaac digged again the wells of water, which they had digged in the days of Abraham his father; for the philistines had stopped them after the death of Abraham: and he called their names after the names by which his father had called them. And Isaac's servants digged in the valley, and found there a well of springing water.*

"And the herdsmen of Gerar did strive with Isaac's herdsmen, saying, the water is ours: and he called the name of the well Esek; because they strove with him."

B) *Esek* means, "Contention." Contention speaks of the enemies' attempt to bring about confusion and strife.

Verse 21 states, *"And they digged another well, and strove for that also: and he called the name of it Sitnah."*

C) *Sitnah* means, "Opposition, Accusation." Same root as Satan the accuser, the adversary. *Sitnah* is the level where the enemy will launch his strongest attack in order to derail the believer from his or her walk with the Lord. He will send strong opposition and accusations because he realizes he could not kill us in the valley, or stop us with contention and strife.

Verse 22 states, *"And he removed from thence, and digged another well; and for that they strove not: and he called the name of it Rehoboth; and he said, For now the LORD hath made room for us, and we shall be fruitful in the land."*

D) *Rehoboth* is from a root that means "to broaden, to enlarge, and to make room." *Rehoboth* is a place of promotion where we begin to blossom and bring forth fruit, because God has enlarged our territory. All the opposition we face before *Rehoboth*, God uses as spiritual muscle builders and fertilizer for our prosperity.

Verse 23 states, *"And he went up from thence to Beer-sheba."*

E) *Beersheba* means, "well of seven," and it comes from the root *Sheba*, which means, "To be complete." *Beersheba* is the ultimate goal for all believers. Look at the two key words used. The well represents the place where water is drawn. Seven is perfection or divine completion. God's destiny for His sons and daughters is divine perfection in Jesus. It is a place of complete spiritual maturity where the flesh is dead, and we are drawing from the wells of salvation as we walk in the fullness of the Holy Spirit.

In John 16:7, Jesus said to his disciples, *"Nevertheless I tell you the truth; it is expedient for you that I go away: for if I go not away, the Comforter will not come unto you; but if I depart, I will send him unto you."* Jesus used a pronoun to describe the Comforter, so we would know that the Comforter is a person. The word Comforter in the Greek is *par-ak-lay-tos*, and it means, "Intercessor, consoler, advocate." He is given to the body of Christ as the Comforter, but his function in the world is different. Jesus said, *"And when he is come, he will reprove the world of sin, and of righteousness, and of judgment"* (John 16:8). Jesus told his disciples that it was expedient for him to go away. The Holy Spirit in him was limitless and without measure, so in-order for the disciples, and believers who would follow, to receive the Holy Spirit, Jesus had to go. The taking away of Jesus to heaven and the sending of the Holy Spirit is the most monumental moment in the history of the church. As a matter of fact, the inception of the church can be traced back to the moment the Holy Spirit arrived. In Luke 24:49, Jesus told his disciples that He would send the promise of his Father upon them, so they should tarry in the city of Jerusalem until they were endued with power from on high. The word endue in the Greek is *en-doo-o*, and it means, "To array, to clothe, to put on." As foresaid, the word power, as it is used in Luke 24:49, is *doo-nam-is*, and it means, "Force, strength, miraculous power." God was going to cover them with strength and power in order to enable them to carry on the work of Jesus on the earth.

The gathering of the followers of Jesus to tarry for the

promise of the Father is recorded in *Acts 2:1–4: "And when the day of Pentecost was fully come, they were all with one accord in one place. And suddenly there came a sound from heaven as of a rushing mighty wind, and it filled all the house where they were sitting. And there appeared unto them cloven tongues like as of fire, and it sat upon each of them. And they were all filled with the Holy Ghost, and began to speak with other tongues, as the Spirit gave them utterance."*

The Father did not pick a random day to send the Holy Spirit to the followers of Jesus. The writer tells us that it was the day of Pentecost. In The Dictionary of Bible and Religion, page 796, William H. Gentz states, "Pentecost, or the Feast of Weeks, as it is called Biblically is the second of three festivals on which every male Jew was required to worship at the temple *(Exodus 34:22–23, II Chronicles 8:12–13)*. The word Pentecost means fifty days, because the feast falls seven weeks after the opening of the harvest season (Leviticus 23:15–16). Sometimes the day is called the Day of First fruits, celebrating the harvest. In the Christian Year it is the fiftieth day after Easter." The Father waited until Jerusalem was filled with devout Jews out of every nation under heaven. When the empowered disciples came out of the upper room speaking in tongues, these men were confounded because they heard them in their native languages. *Acts 2:8–13* states, *"And how hear we every man in our own tongue, wherein we were born?*

"Parthians, and Medes, and Elamites, and the dwellers in Mesopotamia, and in Judaea, and Cappadocia, in Pontus, and Asia, Phrygia, and Pamphylia, in Egypt, and in the parts of Libya about Cyrene, and strangers of Rome, Jews and proselytes, Cretes and Arabians, we do hear them speak in our tongues the wonderful works of God. And they were all amazed, and were in doubt, saying one to another, What meaneth this? Others mocking said, these men are full of new wine."

The mockers were right in saying they were filled with new wine, but wrong in thinking that the wine was the same as the intoxicant men consume to be drunk. Wine is a form of the Holy Spirit, and new wine meant God was filling His people with the Holy Spirit in a manner never seen. When Peter stood up with the eleven to preach the first message of the Spirit-filled church, he said to them, *"For these are not drunken, as you suppose, seeing it is but the third hour of the day"* (Acts 2:15). Peter did not say they were not drunk. He said they were not drunk as the men supposed. They were drunk with the wine of the Spirit. This wine does not leave a person feeling hung-over and sick. This wine gives the believer the strength and power to love their enemies, and to overcome the gates of hell. This is the wine needed by alcoholics, drug addicts, and other addicts trying to pacify themselves with all types of intoxicants.

It is interesting to note the fact that Jesus' first miracle was turning water into wine, and He did it on the third day. The Miracle is recorded in *John 2*. The bridal party ran out of wine. Running out of wine was an embarrassment. Jesus' mother made him aware of the problem.

John 2:5–8 states, *"His mother saith unto the servants, Whatsoever he saith unto you, do it. And there were set there six waterpots of stone, after the manner of the purifying of the Jews, containing two or three firkins apiece. Jesus saith unto them, Fill the waterpots with water. And t hey filled them up to the brim. And he saith unto them, Draw out now, and bear unto the governor of the feast. And they bare it."* Please don't miss this revelation. There were six water pots of stone. Six is the number of Man and Satan. Water pots of stone represent earthen vessels, and the attempt of the Pharisees to be cleansed via ritualistic washing. Two or three firkins are roughly 120 gallons. Remember, there were 120 disciples in the upper room waiting to be endued with power from on high. Jesus told them to "fill the water pots with water." This is a foreshadowing of believers being filled with the Holy Ghost. When the governor of the feast tasted the water, which was turned to wine, he said to the bridegroom, *"Every man at the beginning doth set forth good wine; and when men have well drunk, then that which is worse: but thou hast kept the good wine until now" (John 2:10).* Beloved, you are still alive because Jesus has kept the good wine until now. We are on the verge of a great outpouring of the Spirit of the Lord. As Bishop T.D. Jakes says, "get ready, get ready, get ready."

Peter told the listeners what they saw was a fulfillment of that which was spoken by the Prophet Joel. *"And it shall come to pass in the last days, saith God, I will pour out of my Spirit upon all flesh: and your sons and your daughters shall prophesy, and your young men shall dream dreams: and on my servants and on my handmaidens I will pour out in those days of my Spirit; and they shall prophesy"* (Acts 2:17-18). We don't have to look far to realize we are living in the last days. The enemy is pulling out all his tricks to destroy as many people as he can, but God is filling His sons, His daughters, His servants, and

His handmaidens with His Spirit. The day of the one-man show is over. We are seeing the restoration of the Antioch Church as a model and a paradigm for the triumph of God's people. The Antioch Church is the model that shows us how to flow together as we minister before the Lord. As we minister before Him in unity, the Holy Spirit will manifest with instructions on how to take territory from the Devil, and get people delivered.

Peter told them Jesus of Nazareth was a man approved of God among them by miracles and wonders and signs. He reminded them that they had crucified Him, but God had loosed him from the pains of death. Verse 37 states, *"Now when they heard this, they were pricked in their heart, and said unto Peter and to the rest of the apostles, Men and brethren, what shall we do?"* Keep in mind it was mentioned earlier that the work of the Holy Spirit in the world is to reprove the world of sin, and of righteousness, and of judgment. When the word of God is ministered under the unction of the Holy Spirit, sinners will cry out, "What must we do to be saved?" They will do this because the Holy Spirit will convict them. Once an individual realizes he is convicted, that individual will do anything in order to avoid a prison or death sentence. They will throw themselves on the mercy of the court, pleading for mercy from the judge. Jesus, the righteous judge, has overruled the prosecuting Devil and is waiting to extend mercy. Peter told them to, *"Repent and be baptized in the name of Jesus Christ for the remission of sins, and they would receive the gift of the Holy Ghost"* (Acts 2:38). He told them to baptize in the name of Jesus because all power is in His name. There can be no salvation without repentance, and no baptism of the Holy Spirit without salvation. Peter told them, *"The promise is for them, their children, and all that are afar off, even as many as the Lord our God shall call"* (Acts 2:39).

The Holy Spirit works in us to give us the mind of Christ so we can think on Godly thoughts. He can break the power of the carnal mind, so we no longer have to be slaves to lustful thinking. He works on the mind because the mind controls the body, and thought precedes actions. When I lived in New York City, and frequented nightclubs to satisfy my lust for wine and women, I made the decision earlier in the week as to which club I would attend. When my body arrived at the club, it was only following instructions given to it by a previously made up mind. Individuals trapped in drug addiction, pornography, or any other sin, can delivered by the washing of the blood of Jesus, and the renewing of the mind via the work of the Holy Spirit. Believers must continue to yield to the Holy Spirit, because without Him we will have a form of godliness, but no power. We must fight the encroachment of false doctrine that denies the baptism of the Holy Spirit with the evidence of speaking in tongues. We must endeavor to manifest the fruits of the Spirit in our lives. We must allow the Holy Spirit to deal with our carnal minds so we can receive the mind of Christ.

CHAPTER 7
HAVE YOU LOST YOUR MIND?

Phil 2:5-11 states, *"Let this mind be in you, which was also in Christ Jesus: Who, being in the form of God, thought it not robbery to be equal with God: But made himself of no reputation, and took upon him the form of a servant, and was made in the likeness of men: And being found in fashion as a man, he humbled himself, and became obedient unto death, even the death of the cross. Wherefore God also hath highly exalted him, and given him a name which is above every name: That at the name of Jesus every knee should bow, of things in heaven, and things in earth, and things under the earth; And that every tongue should confess that Jesus Christ is Lord, to the glory of God the Father."*

There is a slogan that has been used by the United Negro College fund for years. The slogan is imbedded in my mind because I have been hearing it since I was a child. The slogan is, "A mind is a terrible thing to waste." We talk about the mind a great deal. When someone articulates something we were thinking about, we say, "You just read my mind." When a person is trying to recall something, they say, "It's in the back of my mind." When we ask someone to do something that seems crazy, the response might be, "You must be out of your 'cotton picking' mind." Random House Webster's Dictionary defines the word mind as, *1) The element, part, or process in a human or other conscious being that reasons, thinks, feels, wills, perceives, judges, etc. 2) Intellect or understanding, especially as distinguished from the emotions and will. 3) The Mind is a philosophical, psychological, and general term for the center of all mental activity, as contrasted with the body and the spirit. The brain is a psychological term for the organic structure that makes mental activity possible.*

In *Romans 12:1–2*, The Apostle writes, *"I beseech you therefore,*

89

brethren, by the mercies of God, that ye present your bodies a living sacrifice, holy, acceptable unto God, which is your reasonable service. And be not conformed to this world: but be ye transformed by the renewing of your mind, that ye may prove what is that good, and acceptable, and perfect, will of God." Paul tells us to give God our bodies as a present. He instructs us to do this because God wants to use it as a temple to tabernacle with us. Like the Old Testament Priests, we are expected by God to present a daily offering to Him. We are to be living sacrifices whereas in the Old Testament, sacrifices were not alive. The Apostle calls the offering of our bodies, "a reasonable service." In the original language, the word is "priestly service." It is connected to the word "present," which is the word for making an offering. The offering of the priest is an act of worship, so the best way to worship God is to offer our bodies as a present to him. Gene Cunningham writes, "In Old Testament times, a lamb was offered every morning and every evening (Ex. 29:39). The morning offering was made at nine o' clock, and the evening offering at 'twilight,' which means 'between the evenings.' This was three o' clock in the afternoon. We can see here that God was teaching Israel to look forward to the coming 'Lamb of God who takes away the sin of the *world, (John 1:29).* At the crucifixion, Jesus hung on the cross during this six-hour period, from day until night *(Psalm. 22:2).* Our Lord declared that if anyone desires to follow Him as a true disciple, he must 'deny himself, and take up his cross daily, and follow me' *(Luke 22:4).* The offering of our life means that we are not our own *(1 Corinthian 6:19–20).* We are no longer to live for ourselves, but for Christ *(2 Corinthian 5:15).* The sacrifices and offerings He wants us to bring are within the reach of each one of us!"[11]

Paul knew it would be impossible for us to give our bodies to God if our minds were not renewed, so he tells us how to present our bodies to God. We must not be conformed to this world's system, because it represents ungodliness. The earth is the Lord's and the fullness thereof, but the world's system belongs to the Devil. Jesus called him the prince of this world. Random House Webster's Collegiate Dictionary defines the word conform as, "to act in accord with the prevailing standards, attitudes, practices, etc., of a society or a group; to be or become similar in form, nature, or character." God wants us to have the attitude, nature, and character of Jesus.

The Apostle tells us to be transformed by the renewing of our mind. The word transformed in the Greek is, *met-am-or-fo-o*, and it means, "to change, or to transfigure." It is the process a moth undergoes to become a butterfly. The word renewing in the Greek is, *an-ak-ah-ee-no-sis*, and it means "renovation." In order for renovation to take place, there has to be some tearing down. There are some worldly things in our minds that the Holy Spirit has to tear down in the renovation process, so we can receive the mind of Christ. Without the mind of Christ, we will not be able to know the perfect will of God. Without the perfect will of God, it will be impossible for us to reach our full potential in Him.

Prior to coming to Christ, our thought process was dominated by sensual pleasures, and those sensual pleasures were done in our bodies. God desires to revamp our thinking so our actions can be Godly. The adversary desires to keep us thinking carnally so our actions will be ungodly. The major part of the warfare against the forces of darkness is in the mind. The enemy wants to set up strongholds in our minds to stop us from discerning the will of God.

A stronghold is a well-fortified place, or a fortress. When someone is addicted to pornography, the Devil sets up a stronghold in his or her mind. This stronghold gives them a physical craving for perverse and promiscuous gratification. Drug addiction is another stronghold or fortress that has some individuals bound. These individuals will do and say anything to satisfy the urges and cravings they feel. Twelve-step programs have their place, but I believe the first step any addict must take is a step towards the deliverance Jesus has provided. Only Jesus can give ultimate victory, because at the root of the problem there are spirits warring against our minds. 2 Corinthians 10:3-5 states, *"For though we walk in the flesh, we do not war after the flesh: (For the weapons of our warfare are not carnal, but mighty through God to the pulling down of strongholds; Casting down imaginations, and every high thing that exalteth itself against the knowledge of God, and bringing into captivity every thought to the obedience of Christ."*

The word carnal in the Greek is *sar-kee-kos*, and it means, "pertaining to the flesh, unregenerate." It comes from the word *sarx*, which means "human nature," with its frailties and passions. It is the part of us that craves sensual pleasures. We must not deceive ourselves into thinking there is anything good in the unregenerate nature of man.

Romans 8:5-8 states, *"For they that are after the flesh do mind the things of the flesh; but they that are after the Spirit the things of the Spirit. For to be carnally minded is death; but to be spiritually minded is life and peace. Because the carnal mind is enmity against God: for it is not subject to the law of God, neither indeed can be. So then they that are in the flesh cannot please God."* The word enmity in the Greek is *ek-thrah*, and it means, "Hostility, a reason for opposition." It comes from the word *ekh-thros* and that word means, "To hate, an adversary (especially Satan)." It does not matter how religious a person appears to be on the outside. If they have a mind that has not been renewed by God through the Blood of Jesus, the indwelling of the Holy Spirit, and the washing of the water of the word, they hate God. I know hate is a strong word, but the Bible says, *"Let God be true and let every man be a liar."* Men seek to create gods that allow them to think and act carnally, yet look and act religious. These men use religion as a cover, but in actuality, they want to get as far away from the true and living God as possible.

In their attempt to appear godly, they set up a religious veneer using idols and other relics in order to deceive those that lack discernment and spiritual insight. Romans 1:22–23 says this about them: *"Professing themselves to be wise, they became fools, and changed the glory of the incorruptible God into an image made like to corruptible man, and to birds, and four-footed beasts, and creeping things."* We must continue to allow the Holy Spirit to teach us the mind of Christ. Anything in us, whether it is in thought, word, or deed, which is not like Jesus, we must ask Him to eradicate.

Warfare is a serious matter, and it is not for the faint of heart. The Bibles says, *"Satan is roaming around like a roaring lion seeking those who he can destroy" (1 Peter 5:8).* Once he gets control of the mind, he can direct the body to do whatever he wants it to do. He will dispatch demons to attack us based on the spiritual level we have attained in Christ. Ephesians 6:12 states, *"Finally, my brethren, be strong in the Lord, and in the power of his might. Put on the whole armor of God that ye may be able to stand against the wiles of the devil. For we wrestle not against flesh and blood, but against principalities, against powers, against the rulers of the darkness of this world, against spiritual wickedness in high places."* The word wiles in the Greek is *meth-od-i-ah*, and it means, "Trickery, to lie in wait." It comes from a compound word, *meta*, which means, "accompaniment, amid," and *hod-yoo-o*, which means, "to travel, to journey." Satan is traveling among us on this road, waiting for an opportune time to attack us.

Job 1:6-7 states, *"Now there was a day when the sons of God came to present themselves before the LORD, and Satan came also among them. And the LORD said unto Satan, Whence comest thou? Then Satan answered the LORD, and said, From going to and fro in the earth, and from walking up and down in it."* Satan is not journeying up and down the Earth because he has nothing better to do. He is looking for an opening or a weak moment so he can pounce like a Lion waiting to devour an unsuspecting prey. He is an adversary that uses stealth as his mode of operation. He does not come yelling and screaming. He is subtle, and he crouches like a lion with a deathly stillness, salivating as he peers at the unsuspecting prey. Jesus knows better than anyone does the trickery of the adversary. He inspired the Apostle Paul to write these words found in 2nd. Corinthians 2:11: *"Lest Satan should get an advantage over us: for we are not ignorant of his devices."* The word devices, or schemes, is the Greek word *no-ay-mah*, and it means, "plots, plans, and stratagem."

When the Apostle says we wrestle, or struggle, the Greek word is *pal-ay*, and it is a term for hand-to-hand combat. This battle is not against flesh and blood, although Satan's gateway into our lives is through people. We must recognize the spirit behind the person and plan our strategy accordingly. We cannot successfully fight against an enemy without first identifying the enemy. Once the enemy is identified, we must determine the arsenal of weapons he is using against us. God has given us what we need to defend ourselves against the enemy and all his representatives. He does not leave us ignorant; He tells us we are locked in hand-to-hand combat with principalities, powers, the rulers of the darkness of this world, and against spiritual wickedness in high places.

The onus is on the believer to be on guard constantly. We must worship, pray, fast, and study the word of God. We must resist the temptation to feed our minds with things that are ungodly. It might require us to stop watching some programs on television, or we might have to stop listening to certain types of music and reading certain magazines. In 1st. John 2:15–16, the Apostle John wrote, *"Love not the world, neither the things that are in the world. If any man loves the world, the love of the Father is not in him.*

For all that is in the world, the lust of the flesh, and the lust of the eyes, and the pride of life, is not of the Father, but is of the world."

Beloved, the Devil does not have any new tricks; he has new people to trick. The same trickery he used on Eve is the same trickery he has used on all her descendants. Let us endeavor to use the weapons God has given us so we may walk in victory and glorify the name of Jesus.

Armor is something that is worn by soldiers, and God has provided the best armor for every soldier in Christ. God cannot wear the armor for us; He has provided the equipment, but we must put it on. When we put it on, we must not leave any part of it off, because as foresaid, the enemy is looking for an opening or an opportune time to launch his next attack. When Jesus defeated the devil in the wilderness, *Luke 4:13* states, *"And when the devil had ended all the temptation, he departed from him for a season."* The New International Version puts it this way: *"When the devil had finished all this tempting, he left him until an opportune time."* The adversary is a persistent foe, and he is always looking for his next opportunity to attack. The armor is important in our ability to attack and withstand the attacks of the enemy, so I take this opportunity to examine the whole armor.

The Armor

1) Our loins must be girt about with truth – Satan is a master manipulator who makes his lies sound like the truth. Jesus called him the father of lies. We must protect the sensitive areas of our defense with the truth. What is the truth? In *John 17:17*, Jesus said, *"Sanctify them through thy truth: thy word is truth."* We must wear the truth of God's word like a strong belt. When the enemy masquerades lies that appear as truth, we will be able to discern his tricks with the truth of Gods word. Anything he brings that opposes God's word is a lie.

2) In his commentary, Matthew Henry says, "Truth is our girdle, this is the strength of our loins; and it girds on all other pieces of our armor, and therefore is first mentioned."

3) The breastplate of righteousness – The breastplate is symbolic of the covering of our heart. Our hearts must be covered with righteousness. Not with self-righteousness but with the righteousness imputed unto us by Jesus. His righteousness protects and fortifies us because the heart is the seat of our emotions, and our trust. The enemy will attack us emotionally and cause us to lose trust in God.

4) Feet shod with the preparation of the gospel of peace – The feet speaks of our walk with Jesus. Gospel means good news; Jesus Christ has come into the world to give us an opportunity to have peace with God. Matthew Henry says, "Shoes, or greaves of brass, were formerly part of the military armor to defend the feet against the gall-traps, and sharp sticks, which were wont to be laid to obstruct the marching of the enemy, those who fell upon them being unfit to march. The preparation of the gospel of peace signifies a resolved frame of heart which will enable us to walk with a steady pace in the way of religion."

5) Shield of faith – The Bible says the shield of faith will help us quench the fiery darts of the wicked. The shield is one of the offensive weapons. The writer to the Hebrews said, *"Without faith it is impossible to please God."* Faith must be the most important part of the armor, because if we lack faith and displease God, the enemy will have his way with us. The Apostle Paul backs this up when he uses the words, "above all." The wicked one will fire fiery darts at us in order to penetrate our shield of faith. When we suffer a great loss, he will try to make us question God by wondering where God was, and why He did not prevent it. When the enemy attacks our shield, we must remember *1 Peter 4:12–13*: *"Beloved, think it not strange concerning the fiery trial which is to try you, as though some strange thing happened unto you: But rejoice, inasmuch as ye are partakers of Christ's sufferings; that, when his glory shall be revealed, ye may be glad also with exceeding joy."*

6) The helmet of salvation – The helmet covers the head, and Jesus has provided salvation for us. The enemy will attempt to make us feel like we are not saved because we mess up at times. Jesus said, *"no one can pluck us out of His*

hand." Our salvation is secure and eternal because it is provided by Jesus.

7) The sword of the Spirit: The word of God – This is the only offensive weapon in the armor given to us by Jesus. We must continue to sharpen our sword because we cannot successfully attack the enemy with a dull sword. We should allow the Holy Spirit to lead us and guide us as we study the word. When we are grounded in the Word of God, it allows us to go on the offensive against the enemy. We must hide the Word in our heart to protect us from sin.

8) In *Psalm 119:105, 11-12*, David wrote, *"Thy word is a lamp unto my feet, and a light unto my path."* *"Thy word have I hid in mine heart, that I might not sin against thee. Blessed art thou, O LORD: teach me thy statutes."*

9) Praying in the spirit – Prayer is the vehicle we use to present our request to God and to receive instructions from Him. We pray in the spirit because the Bible says we do not know what to pray for, or how to pray. The Spirit helps us to pray in the right way because He knows the mind of Christ. We pray in the Holy Spirit utilizing our heavenly language. When we pray in the Spirit, God will reveal the location of the enemy and the strategy we should use to defeat Him. Matthew Henry says, "Prayer must buckle on all the other parts of our Christian armor."

It is interesting to note the fact that there is no armor for our backs. The reason for this is that our backs are taken care of by God. The significance lies in the fact that God does not want us to be revisionist in our dealings with the enemy. We are to be on the offensive, raiding the camp of the enemy and taking souls captive for the Kingdom of our Lord. We will suffer some casualties, but we must remember the word of the Apostle Paul, who said, *"to live is Christ but to die is gain."* We will suffer tribulation in this life, but Jesus has won the ultimate victory for us, and as long as we keep Him as Captain of the Host, we are assured victory. Victory will come at a cost, and the cost is that we will have to spend some time in the wilderness so God can prepare us for His Glory.

CHAPTER 8
DON'T DIE IN THE WILDERNESS

Song of Solomon 8:5a: *"Who is this that cometh up from the wilderness, leaning upon her beloved?"* Every born again believer must go through what I call "wilderness experiences." Random House Webster's Collegiate Dictionary defines the word wilderness as, "A wild, uncultivated, uninhabited region, as a forest or desert." When the Lord called us out of darkness into His marvelous light, we did not receive instant sanctification. We came out of the world's system into the Church of Jesus Christ with some ungodly thoughts and habits. God, in his infinite wisdom, has chosen the wilderness experiences of our lives to purge us of our carnal thoughts and ungodly actions.

Human beings do not appear to learn the majority of life's valuable lessons in times of prosperity and bliss. We seem to be like muscles in that we need friction and resistance in order to grow. Jesus is the Bridegroom, and He is perfecting His people to be His bride. The bride of Jesus will not be prepared for Him in some fine palace surrounded by courtiers but will receive preparation in the wilderness and the furnace of affliction.

There is no exemption or deferment for the believer from their wilderness experience. Everyone that names the name of Jesus will find himself or herself going in, or coming out of the wilderness. *Deuteronomy 8:2* sums up the purpose of the wilderness beautifully. In speaking to the children of Israel, Moses said, *"And thou shalt remember all the way which the LORD thy God led thee these forty years in the wilderness, to humble thee, and to prove thee, to know what was in thine heart, whether thou wouldest keep his commandments, or no."*

The purpose of the wilderness is to humble us, and to prove to us what is actually in our hearts. We show people the side of us we want them to see, but there are hidden, dark places in all our hearts and God has to deal with those areas in order to get us to a place of perfection in Christ. The amount of time we spend in a particular wilderness will be determined by how willing we are to yield to the teachings of the Lord.

Solomon asked a very important question about the identity of the individuals coming out of the wilderness leaning upon the arm of their beloved. We know that the beloved is none other than the Lord Jesus, but who is doing the leaning? It is a remnant washed in the blood of the lamb, and birthed in the furnace of affliction. It is important to note that only a remnant came out of the wilderness after the exodus. Many of God's people died there because of their murmuring and complaining. It is also important to note the fact that the Bible teaches about five wise virgins and five foolish virgins. The five foolish virgins, who were not prepared when the bridegroom came, were not unbelievers, because virgins are never considered unbelievers in the Bible. They represent believers who had not yielded to the Holy Spirit's attempt to prepare them for the coming of the Bridegroom. The wilderness is a place of preparation for the bride of Jesus. The theme of a remnant is prevalent throughout the scriptures. Abram was called to leave his kindred and his father's house. Moses was separated from his brethren from birth. Out of all of David's brothers, he was the one chosen and anointed to be king. Joseph was his father's favorite, and was hated by his brothers.

Jesus had his own wilderness experience, and this should be a confirmation to all believers that no one is exempt. *Matthew 3:16–17* states, *"And Jesus, when he was baptized, went up straightway out of the water: and, lo, the heavens were opened unto him, and he saw the Spirit of God descending like a dove, and lighting upon him: And lo a voice from heaven, saying, This is my beloved Son, in whom I am well pleased."* This event has to be considered as one of the greatest events anyone could've experienced. The Spirit came down and filled Jesus in preparation for His ministry. His Father is heard from Heaven expressing His pleasure in His beloved Son. In the next chapter Matthew states, *"Then was Jesus led up of the Spirit into the wilderness to be tempted of the devil."* Mark 1:12 reads, *"And immediately the Spirit driveth him into the wilderness."*

Jesus had no imperfection or sin in Him. His journey into the wilderness took place so He could experience every temptation

98

the adversary would use in his attack against us. His wilderness experience was exacerbated by the fact that He fasted forty days and forty nights. Forty is the number in scripture that typifies testing, trials, and probation. According to Evangelist Ed. F. Vallowe, there are eight great periods of testing revealed in the word of God; since eight is the number of new beginnings, it is safe to say we will come out of each wilderness experience with an anointing to operate on a new dimension.

1) Moses was in the mountain of Sinai 40 days and nights receiving the Law (Exodus 24:18).
2) Moses' departure represented Forty days of testing for the Israelites. They failed when they made Aaron fashion a golden calf for them to go before them as a god.
3) For their rebellion, God tried them in the wilderness for Forty years (Numbers 14:34).
4) The Prophet Elijah spent Forty days in Horeb after his experience on Mt. Carmel. The Bible states, *"And he arose, and did eat and drink, and went in the strength of that meat Forty days and Forty nights unto Horeb the mount of God."*
5) Forty days Jonah preached judgment would come to the city of Nineveh *(Jonah 3:4).*
6) Forty days Ezekiel laid on his right side to symbolize the Forty years of Judah's transgression *(Ezekiel 4:6).*
7) We mention at the outset that Jesus was in the wilderness forty days and forty nights.
8) Forty days Jesus was seen of His disciples, speaking of the things pertaining to the Kingdom of God. Acts 1:3 states, *"To whom also he shewed himself alive after His passion by many infallible proofs, being seen of them Forty days, and speaking o the things pertaining to the Kingdom of God."*

If you are experiencing a wilderness experience right now, be encouraged because Jesus defeated our enemy in the wilderness and came out with anointing and power. You can do the same thing if you allow God to humble you and teach you in the midst of it. 1 Corinthian 10:13 states, *"There hath no temptation taken you but such as is common to man: but God is faithful, who will not suffer you to be tempted above that ye are able; but will with the temptation also make a way to escape, that ye may be able to bear it."*

The gospel writer tells us that Jesus was hungry after fasting forty days and forty nights. Anyone who has every fasted can identify with the hunger pangs felt as a result of going without food for a sustained period of time. It appears Jesus went without food and water, so His fast was definitely a tough one. Matthew 4:3 states, *"And when the tempter came to him, he said, if thou be the Son of God, command that these stones be made bread."*

It is not a matter of *if*, but *when*, the tempter will come. While we are in the wilderness, the tempter will attempt to entice us to turn from God, but we must be steadfast. He will come at our lowest moment. He did not visit Jesus until Jesus was hungry, and he knew exactly what to tempt Jesus with, because he questions Jesus' identity and tells Him to turn the stones into bread. He knows our fleshly appetites, so he will tempt us with something with which we are struggling. We can all learn from Jesus in terms of how he responded to the tempter. Jesus said, *"It is written, man shall not live by bread alone, but by every word that proceedeth out of the mouth of God."* It is imperative that we not only learn the word but also obey the word. The tempter tried to use scripture to entice Jesus, by quoting a portion of *Deuteronomy 8:3*. The Devil is not averse to using the Word of God as a way of enticing us. The only way we can overcome him is to know and obey the word.

The life of David is a great example to every believer of the tests and trials we will experience before we come into the fullness of what God has ordained us to be. David was anointed to be King of Israel, but he did not go straight to the palace for a coronation. He returned to the fields to feed his father's sheep. We live in a society and a world where we want things to be done right away, but when God has a calling on our lives, He takes us through a process to get us ready to fulfill that calling. When David goes to the palace for the first time, he goes because the reigning King needs a musician to soothe his soul from the torment that ensued when the spirit of the Lord departed from him. When a Philistine giant named Goliath challenges King Saul and the armies of Israel, David volunteers to fight the giant. *1st Samuel 17:16* states, *"And the Philistine drew near morning and evening, and presented himself forty days."* I remind the reader the number forty represents testing and probation. A Philistine is a type of giant every believer will have to face to get to his or her next dimension in God. The number forty signifies the fact that we will be tested by giants in our walk with Jesus. We can learn a great deal from David's approach to his battle with the giant called Goliath.

When David finds out that the giant Goliath has come up against Israel, he asked this question: *"Who is this uncircumcised Philistine, that he should defy the armies of the living God" (1ˢᵗ. Samuel 17:26)*. Circumcision was given to the nation of Israel as a sign of the covenant they had with God. When God established the covenant with Abraham, it was a blood covenant. The covenant was irrevocable, and meant that the enemies of Abraham's descendants were God's enemies. The covenant was so important, *Hebrews 6:13* states, *"For when God made promise to Abraham, because He could swear by no greater, He swears by Himself."* You and I were brought into that covenant because of the finished work of the Lord Jesus. David knew the Israelites were not just any army, but the army of the living God. We have a blood covenant with God that was ratified by the Blood of Jesus. This covenant can't be annulled. As you face your trials, let the enemy know that you have a blood covenant.

Armed with the knowledge that the Philistine did not have a covenant with the living God, David decides to go to battle against him. King Saul offers David his armor, but he refused to use the king's armor because he had not proved it. Remember, the Bible says, *"the weapons of our warfare are not carnal but mighty through God for the pulling down of strongholds"* (2ⁿᵈ. Corinthians 10:4). Our chief weapon is the name of Jesus. David decided to battle the giant with a sling and five smooth stones.

This paints a wonderful picture of the grace of God and its necessity for a victorious life. The Philistine giant ridiculed David because David was young, but David responded by saying, *"Thou comest to me with a sword, and with a spear, and with a shield: but I come to thee in the name of the LORD of hosts, the God of the armies of Israel, whom thou hast defied. This day will the LORD deliver thee into mine hand; and I will smite thee, and take thine head from thee; and I will give the carcasses of the host of the Philistines this day unto the fowls of the air, and to the wild beasts of the earth; that all the earth may know that there is a God in Israel. And all this assembly shall know that the LORD saveth not with sword and spear: for the battle is the Lord's, and he will give you into our hands"* (1.st Sam 17:45–47). David is not looking to take credit for himself. He gives glory to God by publicly stating that the battle is the Lord's, and the Lord would deliver the Philistine into their hands.

He is able to defeat the giant, and gains favor in the sight of the King who sets him over the men of war. David never allowed his victories and his anointing to puff him up. *"David went out wherever Saul sent him, and behaved himself wisely: and Saul set him over the men of war, and he was accepted in the sight of all the people, and also in the sight of Saul's servants"* (1ˢᵗ. Samuel 18:5). David's humility and his love for God led to his promotion.

It is a good example of how an individual should conduct his or herself as part of the body of Christ. David does not act arrogant and pompous because he defeated the giant and has favor in the eyes of the King, and rightfully so. We must endeavor to remain humble when promoted, because promotion brings with it many challenges, as David is about to find out. In his new role as leader of the men of war, David would accompany King Saul on the battlefield, and Saul turned against David because David handled himself well on the battlefield and received praise from the women. *1ˢᵗ. Samuel 18:6–9* states, *"And it came to pass as they came, when David was returned from the slaughter of the Philistine, that the women came out of all cities of Israel, singing and dancing, to meet king Saul, with tabrets, with joy, and with instruments of music. And the women answered one another as they played, and said, Saul hath slain his thousands, and David his ten thousands. And Saul was very wroth, and the saying displeased him; and he said, 'They have ascribed unto David ten thousands, and to me they have ascribed but thousands: and what can he have more but the kingdom?' And Saul eyed David from that day and forward."*

From this point on, the King tried to destroy David, but David would not lift a finger against him. David has to flee to the cave of Adullam. *Adullam* means "refuge." *Micah 1:15* calls the city, *"the glory of Israel."* David flees to a beautiful city that is a refuge, but he is unable to enjoy the beauty of the city because he has to dwell in a cave. The Hebrew word for cave is *meh-aw-raw*, and it means "a cavern, a den, a hole." It comes from the root word *oor*, and this word means "to be bare, to be made naked." In the perfection process, God will strip us of everything that is not like Jesus until we become so transparent the image of Jesus is evident in us. Another meaning of the root word *oor* is, "to open the eyes, to wake, to lift up."

If hiding in a cave wasn't bad enough, David had to take responsibility for the members of his father's household. *1ˢᵗ. Samuel 22:1–2* states, *"David therefore departed thence, and escaped to the cave Adullam: and when his brethren and all his father's house heard it, they went down to him. And every one that was in distress, and every one that was in debt, and every one that was discontented, gathered themselves unto him; and he became a captain over them: and there were with him about four hundred men."* God was teaching David how to lead from the ground up. He would sit in the seat of the king one day, and God wanted to make sure David would be able to identify with the people, no matter what their condition.

David was able to survive his wilderness experiences and ascend the throne of Israel. God is no respecter of persons, and he wants you to be victorious in your wilderness experiences. Whatever situation you are facing right now, do not faint or lose heart. God is going to work it into His larger plan for your life, and you will be victorious. Do not listen to the lies of the enemy, which may try to convince you that God has forgotten you. God has you right in the palm of His hands, and your steps are ordered. Do not murmur or complain; it is time to show your faith by praising and giving Him thanks right in the midst of your wilderness. You are coming out, and you are coming out leaning on the arm of your beloved Jesus.

ENDNOTES

1...Gene Cunningham, The Basics: A Categorical Bible Study (Bigelow, AR: American Inland Mission, Inc. 1988), 175

2...Cunningham (The Basics), 172

3...Gene Cunningham, Rivers of Living Water (Hot Springs, Arkansas: Basic Training Bible Ministries, 2006), 23

4...Cunningham (The Basics), 208-211

5...Cunningham (The Basics), 250

6...R.C. Sproul, The Character of God: previously published as One Holy Passion (Nashville, TN: Thomas Nelson Publishers, 1987), 121

7...F.F. Bruce, Tyndale New Testament Commentaries: Revised Edition (Grand Rapids, Michigan: William B. Erdmans Publishing Company, 1st ed. 1963, Reprinted 1997), 109

8...Bruce, 109

9...Sproul, 43

10...Cunningham (The Basics), 2

11...Cunningham (The Basics), 2-3

12...Matthew Henry, Commentary On the Whole Bible (Grand Rapids, Michigan: Zondervan Publishing House, 1961), 1922.

BIBLIOGRAPHY

Bruce, F.F. Tyndale New Testament Commentaries (Romans). Grand Rapids, Michigan: Wm. B. Erdmans Publishing Co. 1985.

Cunningham, Gene. The basics: A Categorical Bible Study. Bigelow, AR: American Inland Mission, Inc. 1990

Cunningham, Gene. Rivers of Living Water. Hot Springs, AR: Basic Training Bible Ministries, 2006

Gentz, William H. The Dictionary of Bible and Religion. Nashville: Abingdon Press, 1986

Henry, Matthew. Comentary On the Whole Bible. Zondervan Publishing House: 1961

Sproul, R.C. The Character of God: Previously published as One Holy Passion. Ann Arbor: Thomas Nelson Publishers, 1987

Strong, James. The New Strongs Exhaustive Concordance of The Bible. Nashville: Thomas Nelson, Inc. 1995

Vallowe, Ed. F. Biblical Mathematics: Keys to Scripture Numerics. Forest Park: ED. F. Vallowe Evangelistic Association, 1995

CPSIA information can be obtained
at www.ICGtesting.com
Printed in the USA
FFOW03n0726280917
40344FF